Jonathan Edwards
AND THE
GOSPEL OF LOVE

Jonathan Edwards

AND THE
GOSPEL OF LOVE

Ronald Story

University of Massachusetts Press
Amherst and Boston

LC 2012026785
ISBN 978-1-55849-983-6 (paper); 982-9 (hardcover)

Designed by Jack Harrison
Set in Adobe Garamond Pro with Albertus display
Printed and bound by Thomson-Shore

Library of Congress Cataloging-in-Publication Data

Story, Ronald.
Jonathan Edwards and the gospel of love / Ronald Story.
p. cm.
Includes bibliographical references (p.   ) and indexes.
ISBN 978-1-55849-983-6 (pbk. : alk. paper) —
ISBN 978-1-55849-982-9 (library cloth : alk. paper)
1. Edwards, Jonathan, 1703-1758.   I. Title.
BX7260.E3S764 2012
285.8092—dc23
2012026785

British Library Cataloguing in Publication data are available.

To
William R. Taylor
and
the late Robert Griffith,

MENTORS

Contents

Preface

This book is the latest chapter in a lengthy personal effort to discover the real Jonathan Edwards. I first encountered Edwards as an undergraduate at the University of Texas in the late 1950s, where we read, or were at least exposed to, his sermon "Sinners in the Hands of an Angry God." At the time he sounded entirely familiar. I grew up in a Southern Baptist tradition where preachers sounded a similar tocsin of human depravity, implacable damnation, and everlasting torment. On the basis of this one stunning sermon and having had enough for the moment of pulpit-induced fear and guilt, I set Edwards aside.

My next exposure came in graduate school at the University of Wisconsin in the 1960s, where I encountered the arguments of Perry Miller and others that Puritan ministers were powerful intellectual figures with a strong corporate mindset and, even more, that Jonathan Edwards, though a Puritan, was a modern thinker who grasped the implications of Newton and Locke as few New England contemporaries did. Moreover, he seemed, some said, to have influenced the coming of the American Revolution by helping to foment the Great Awakening. He therefore became a more interesting figure.

But for all this he still remained for most historians, including me, essentially the Calvinist of the "Sinners" sermon, so that when I prepared, with the help of Paul Boller, Jr., the first edition of *A More Perfect Union: Documents in U.S. History* for publication in 1984, I naturally chose to represent Edwards with none other than "Sinners in the Hands of an Angry God." I continued to include this sermon in the next four editions, right through the 5th in the year 2000.

A More Perfect Union unexpectedly became one of the top-selling documentary collections for college undergraduates, gaining sales with every edition—with the result that I became, in this curious way, instrumental in sustaining Edwards's reputation as a brimstone revivalist. Few adopters complained, and my mostly Roman Catholic and Jewish students had little interest anyway. Meanwhile I continued to teach and publish in the cultural, social, and political history of the nineteenth and twentieth centuries rather than the colonial era and was content to do so.

But one Sunday morning in the late 1990s my son and I were strolling in Northampton and happened to pass First Churches, where a service was about to begin on the site, as I knew, of Edwards's own church. We went in, liked the minister, Peter Ives, and the loveliness of the place, and eventually joined the congregation. Reverend Ives learned that I taught American history at the University of Massachusetts just over the Connecticut River, and asked if I would be interested in giving the sermon on the annual Edwards day at First Churches.

I said yes and began to study some of the volumes of Yale University Press's magisterial ongoing new edition of Edwards's writings. Most important for me personally was the sermon series *Charity and Its Fruits,* with its beautiful finale, "Heaven Is a World of Love," a sermon that revealed an Edwards of a complexity and compassion that I had little imagined, in part because not many Edwards scholars, certainly not Perry Miller, had mentioned it. A close second was *A History of the Work of Redemption,* based on sermons delivered just after the *Charity* sermons. There were also volumes containing unfamiliar sermons from the 1720s and early 1730s that seemed to foreshadow Edwards's mature views and lay out new paths in a way I did not expect.

The sermon I delivered still quoted "Sinners" and referenced judgmental Calvinism. But it also quoted "Heaven." By 2003, when I was asked to preach on the occasion of the 300th anniversary of Edwards's birth, I highlighted almost exclusively the Edwards of *Charity* and "Love" as representing the Edwards I was coming to know far better than "Sinners" did. I was also finding some confirmation in the trove of Edwards sermons and writings continuing to issue from Yale, particularly Stephen Stein's magnificent editions of Edwards's biblical notes and commentaries, and in the work of Gerald McDermott, Roland Delattre, Mark Valeri, and other scholars, even though few tacked in quite the direction I seemed headed.

The 2003 sermon grew into an essay in Dr. Kerry Buckley's fine collection of articles on the history of Northampton, which in turn led Dr. Herbert Richardson to suggest that I turn the essay into a book. I am indebted to Herbert Richardson for suggesting the book and to Kerry Buckley for requesting the essay. Most of all, I am indebted to Reverend Peter Ives, who gave me the opportunity to preach on Edwards. No kinder, more considerate, more devout, more dedicated individual than Peter Ives has ever graced the pulpit that stands where Jonathan Edwards held forth. I hope the three of them find something here of value.

But I feel indebted for another reason, too. In *A More Perfect Union,* I replaced "Sinners" with a selection that more accurately captures the Edwards I have come to know: an excerpt from "Heaven Is a World of Love." That did not quite compensate for the previous five editions, however, so I felt a persistent pang of guilt. *Jonathan Edwards and the Gospel of Love* is therefore, in some sense, my atonement for having helped perpetuate an unfair and misleading stereotype of a remarkable man whose lessons of charity, community, and love we need now more than ever.

And there is much work to be done. My late learned father-in-law, a prominent university professor of American literature, considered Edwards little more than the man responsible for showing preachers how to "leave 'em rolling in the dust." He was highly dubious of this project. I recently had lunch with three accomplished American historians who have published more than a dozen books, several of them prize winners. To a person, they viewed Edwards through the lens of "Sinners" and were likewise dubious that I or anyone could make a compelling alternative case.

These and other experiences suggest that the struggle of McDermott and others to bring clearer readings of Edwards to light has had only modest success to date even among high-ranking academics, never mind the general public. So fixed a reputation will not easily give way, as a glance at how Edwards appears in current textbooks makes clear. As is true of much specialized modern scholarship, some of the new work may simply be too tentative or too cloistered to win over a broad audience, a fate that may await this book as well, though I have struggled against it.

There is in any case much to do and much need to do it. This is my small contribution.

Jonathan Edwards
AND THE
GOSPEL OF LOVE

1

LIFE

JONATHAN EDWARDS is by now the most illustrious resident in the history of the town of Northampton, no small achievement for a little community that has harbored Calvin Coolidge, Sylvia Plath, Sojourner Truth, Sylvester Graham, and George Bancroft. Edwards trumps them all. He may be for us today one of the three or four most illustrious men in the history of pre-Revolutionary New England, standing with John Winthrop, Roger Williams, and Cotton Mather. For enduring influence, he may trump these figures as well. Here are highlights of his life and career.[1]

1703: Born in East Windsor, Connecticut, to Timothy Edwards, a formidable Congregational minister, and Esther Stoddard Edwards, the daughter of the even more formidable Solomon Stoddard, the Congregational pastor of Northampton, Massachusetts. One of eleven Edwards children (the rest are girls), Jonathan studies a classical track with his father, who teaches other local children to supplement his ministerial salary. Nine of his sisters attend finishing school in Boston; of the eight who marry, four become the wives of ministers.

1716: Enters the Connecticut Collegiate School, later Yale College; obtains the bachelor's degree in 1720; delivers the valedictory address, and begins graduate work. He studies Locke, Newton, and other modern philosophers and theologians, obtains a graduate degree from Yale in 1722, and serves as a Yale tutor from 1724 to 1726. In later years he attends frequent Yale commencements, gives a commencement address in 1741, and receives Yale graduates and students in his home despite quarreling with the Yale authorities over doctrinal matters.

1719: Contracts severe pleurisy, the first of many illnesses over his life, including collapses in 1725 and again in 1729, when he loses his voice; in

1735 when he takes recuperative leave; and in the 1750s when fever lays him very low. Acquaintances find him "gaunt" and "infirm" before he reaches age forty and "skeletal" at fifty, a condition he is aware of but that his grinding workaholic habits and abstemious diet may exacerbate.

1721: Undergoes a profound and hard-won conversion that brings a consciousness of grace and an apprehension of the sublime beauty and overwhelming power of God. This permanently shapes his sense of true Christianity. He recounts this experience, upon request, in a "Personal Narrative" written in 1740.

1722: Ministers to a Presbyterian congregation in New York City until 1723 when he leaves to assume a brief Congregational pastorate in Bolton, Connecticut. Until 1726 he preaches, while serving as a tutor at Yale, in various area pulpits, including intermittently in Glastonbury, Connecticut.

1722: Begins lifelong "Miscellanies" notebooks, to which he adds "Notes on Scripture" in 1724 and the "Blank Bible" in 1730. These three compilations of notes become Edwards's main repositories for doctrinal and social observation, analysis, and speculation. Also in 1722 he starts another lifelong effort, a "Catalogue" of the books that he purchases, reads, finds of interest, or lends out.

1723: Begins courtship of Sarah Pierpont, the teenage daughter of a prominent New Haven minister, and writes a famous idealizing "Apostrophe" to Sarah's lovely spirituality. They marry in 1727 and have eleven children between 1728 and 1750, all but three of them girls, all but one destined to outlive both parents. The daughters receive sound educations, including "finishing" in Boston; several become the wives of ministers. The boys graduate from Princeton rather than Yale; one, Jonathan Jr., enters the ministry. Sarah, besides mothering a large brood and running a complicated household, comes to figure prominently in Edwards's writings about the spirituality of revivalism.

1727: Moves with Sarah to Northampton, Massachusetts, a farm community on the Connecticut River, as assistant minister to Solomon Stoddard, the illustrious and autocratic leader of the Connecticut Valley churches. Following Stoddard's death in 1729, Edwards accepts an offer to become Northampton's minister. He thus ascends to one of the most significant pulpits, by virtue of the town's size and regional influence, its willingness to pay its minister well, and Stoddard's lingering luster, in all of interior New England.

1730: Begins fully to articulate the social implications of his faith with sermons in the next few years on topics that he had previously touched upon. Among them are "The Dangers of Decline," "Envious Men," "The Duty of Charity to the Poor," and "The State of Public Affairs." These stress, inter alia, the importance of loving both God and man, humanity's God-given social nature, the gospel injunction to help the poor without stint, the iniquity of corrupt and uncaring rulers, the sin of greed and self-serving, strife and contention as destroyers of community, and God's promise to bless collective holiness. He reiterates these themes in later preaching and writing—in, for example, the *Charity and Its Fruits* sermon series of 1738 and reflections on *The Nature of True Virtue* near the end of his life.

1731: Highlights God's omnipotence in "God Glorified in the Work of Redemption, by the Greatness of Man's Dependence upon him," a sermon delivered before dignitaries and ministers in Boston that becomes his first publication and adds to his stature as a leading young exemplar of Puritan doctrine. He recapitulates this notion in many sermons and treatises of the next two decades.

1731: Makes the acquaintance of Boston-area ministers, which brings easier access to books and periodicals and additional contacts with British Reformed preachers and writers. Edwards travels frequently over the years, most commonly (by horseback, in all weathers, often alone) to Kittery, Portsmouth, New Haven, New York, Providence, and various Connecticut Valley and central Massachusetts towns, and to Boston more than a dozen times, including in 1751 to have his portrait painted.

1734: Preaches "A Divine and Supernatural Light, Immediately Imparted to the Soul by the Spirit," later published, which urges the opening of the heart as well as the mind, the feelings as well as the intellect, to the transformative miracle of unearned grace. This and other emotional sermons help foment the "Connecticut Valley Revival," a year-long burst of intense spiritual fervor in Northampton and nearby Massachusetts and Connecticut communities. Edwards's *Faithful Narrative* (1737), a description of the revival's progress and effects, increases his fame in Europe as well as America.

1737: Excluded by church officials from planning for a new meeting house that privileges wealth and diminishes the pulpit in the organization and assignment of pews. This is the first of a series of episodes that reflect and feed town-minister tensions, including the appointment in 1740 of a committee on "matters of difficulty," the drafting of a written covenant in 1742 pledging Christian economic behavior, a "bad book" affair in 1744 that alienates several families, and a confrontation in 1749 over access to the sacraments, including communion.

1738: Preaches "Love the Sum of All Virtue" and "Heaven Is a World of Love," bookend pieces of a twelve-part series on charity and holiness that he delivers while promoting a church charitable fund to supplement the provincial law mandating welfare support. The next year he preaches sermons that will become *A History of the Work of Redemption,* a thirty-part series on human history from the Creation to the Second Coming. These sermons underscore not only the Fall, the Redemption, and the punishment of the minions of Antichrist but also Solomon's Israel as a covenanted nation, Jesus Christ as a poor laboring man, the communitarianism of the early Christians, and the spiritual and material blessings of the earthly Millennium that will precede the Apocalypse.

1740: Begins a ten-year cluster of ministerial ordination and funeral sermons for neighboring parishes. These treat ministers as heroic figures who preach God's word, touch hearts, save souls, and articulate a vision of holy society, and who therefore deserve whole-hearted congregational support, including a fixed salary, a bone of contention in Northampton and elsewhere in this period. The sermons are partly a response to revivalism, which shakes the settled ministry, and partly a response to the displacement of ministers by merchants in the social order, a concern of ministers throughout New England and a central tension of Edwards's career.

1740: Active in the Great Awakening revivals that sweep through colonial North America. Edwards welcomes the British evangelist George Whitefield to Northampton, where the Awakening peaks in late 1741 shortly after Edwards preaches his well-known hellfire sermon "Sinners in the Hands of an Angry God." He writes three additional works on revivalism, including *Religious Affections* (1746), a revisionist treatise drawn from a sermon series in 1743 that rejects inner enthusiasm as a sign of grace in favor of sustained outer behavior on behalf of God and man.

1745: Preaches "The Duties of Christians in a Time of War" in support of a British military expedition against the French at Cape Breton Island, a blow, in Edward's view, against France, the chief Roman Catholic power in the world and the main threat to British and therefore Protestant security in North America. Edwards, though a preacher of harmony and love, reiterates his support of British arms over the next decade, a reflection of the tide of British patriotism that sweeps the colonies and the rising anxiety over a crescendo of raids by France's Indian allies. Frontier warfare is particularly intense in the late 1740s and the mid-1750s, with numerous refugees, many casualties killed or captured, the Edwards parsonage fortified, and the Edwards daughters packed off to Long Island beyond harm's way.

1747: Joins effort originating in Scotland to encourage a global Concert of Prayer among the trans-Atlantic faithful in order to hasten the coming of the evangelical age leading to the Millennium, an effort that he explains and defends in sermons and in *An Humble Attempt to . . . Advance Christ's Kingdom on Earth,* published in 1748. Also in 1747 Edwards welcomes young missionary David Brainerd into his home, praises his work with the Indians, and publishes a biography of Brainerd following his death that year, a further sign of his concern to spread the gospel and move ultimately toward the Millennium.

1750: Dismissed as pastor of Northampton on the grounds that he is excluding people from the sacraments who do not profess their conversion experience and lead sanctified lives. Edwards responds, in *An Humble Inquiry [on] Complete Standing and Full Communion,* that professions of faith for admission to the sacraments must include evidence of holy behavior such as visible love to God and to one another, which had been his basic message for nearly fifteen years. The church council in charge is unyielding. Edwards takes his leave in a "Farewell Sermon" in July 1750, observing to friends that his main supporters (women, the young, the less educated) have had no voice in the affair.

1751: Accepts mission post as minister and instructor to the Indians and British settlers of Stockbridge, Massachusetts, in the Berkshire hills on the frontier. Besides dutifully preaching and teaching, Edwards also manages over the next six years to write treatises on *Freedom of the Will* and *Original Sin,* published in 1754 and 1758 respectively, and on true virtue and God's purpose in the creation, works that together will eventually win much attention from theologians and philosophers.

1757: Accepts presidency of the College of New Jersey, later Princeton. Edwards travels to New Jersey to assume the presidency in February 1758, but falls ill from complications following a smallpox inoculation and dies in late March. He leaves a modest estate, consisting chiefly of funds to educate his children and a library of nearly a thousand books, pamphlets, and personal writings which he bequeaths to his son Jonathan Jr., a minister in the making.

1765: Publication of Edwards's treatises *The Nature of True Virtue* and *The End for Which God Created the World* and a separate volume of sermons. These are followed over the next twenty years by *A History of the Work of Redemption* and volumes containing extracts of *Theological Controversies* from the "Miscellanies" notebooks and additional collections of sermons. In the early nineteenth century there are five multivolume editions of Edwards works plus *Charity and Its Fruits* in 1851 and a selection of *Unpublished Writings* in 1865. Edwards's *Life of David Brainerd* becomes, in many editions and reprintings, one of the most widely distributed books of the century.

1957: *Freedom of the Will* published as volume one of a major new twenty-six-volume edition of Edwards's collected writings from Yale University Press, each volume with the full panoply of modern scholarly and editorial support. Many older editions are reprinted, along with new collections of unpublished sermons and other writings. The Yale Center for Edwards Studies digitizes virtually the whole of the extant Edwards oeuvre for online display, vastly expanding opportunities for scholarly work.

Today divinity schools, departments of history and literature, the entire Protestant world, and to some degree Christendom itself know of Jonathan Edwards. Given the immense array of resources now at our command and the continuing interest across a great range of concerns and disciplines, we will doubtless come to understand him more fully with each passing year.

☼ 2 ☼
PERSONAE

God cannot be made synonymous with the essence of reason or of life or of power, nor with the more popular modern conceptions of limits or of transcendence or of the future. God is what He wills Himself to be.

— KARL BARTH

"JONATHAN EDWARDS divided men in his lifetime," says biographer Iain Murray, "and to no less degree he continues to divide his biographers. . . . The nature of his greatness, the significance of his life and thought, an assessment of his character and writings—on all these, and much else, judgments are divided." One recent scholar sees Edwards as theologian, cosmologist, aesthete, reformer, and social and psychological analyst—a typically varied and largely correct though incomplete assessment that reflects, says another student, Edwards's pronounced "intellectual and spiritual elusiveness."[1]

In much of the historical literature, four images of Edwards loom especially large: Edwards as an intellectual, as a revivalist, as a Calvinist, and as (an encompassing term for an overarching impression) a scold. So strong are these images among the broad literate and academic public that even the quite different and diverse scholarly explorations of the past thirty years seem to have had only modest effect on them. They should therefore serve as a reasonable springboard into the heart of this present examination.

Perry Miller, whose 1949 biography of Edwards may be said to have inaugurated the late twentieth-century wave of scholarly study, saw him as the quintessential lonely intellectual, a frontier pastor nurtured in the Calvinist tradition who also read Locke and Newton, saw the need to reconcile their insights to Calvinist precepts, and spent his life attempting to do precisely that. Having lived through a ghastly global depression

7

and ghastlier global war, Miller admired Edwards's skepticism about the American faith, including what Miller took to be mainstream twentieth-century religious faith, in intrinsic human goodness, the efficacy of reason, wealth as the measure of excellence, and the inevitability of national progress. At some level Miller, though a nonbeliever, saw in Edwards a kind of "dark angel" standing athwart the creed of perpetual improvement, a view that, though only partially correct, was shared by the glum proponents of a mid-twentieth-century school of theological orthodoxy. A Harvard scholar awash in a culture of Babbitry and materialism, Miller also, perhaps especially, admired Edwards as an exemplar of the life of the mind against all odds, struggling for understanding, grappling with non-utilitarian Ultimate Questions. And it must be said that Miller seemed particularly impressed that Edwards led the life of the mind in a backwoods town like Northampton rather than in, say, Cambridge.

Miller's depiction of Edwards as a modern thinker no longer carries the whole scholarly field, not least in its neglect of the tenacious hold over Edwards of Christian faith and the Bible. "The Edwards who emerges in Miller," says Donald Weber, "is a figure unnaturally forced into a variety of modernist poses that simply cannot be defended. Miller claimed too much."[2] Yet despite many revisions, Miller's view of Edwards as a great thinker and writer, a figure representing more than rigid Calvinism and damnation preaching, has partially endured. The modern Yale edition of Edwards's writings, following Miller's lead, treated him from the outset in the 1950s first and foremost as a theologian and philosopher. The first volumes of the Yale series were not sermons, for example, but the treatises *Freedom of the Will, Religious Affections,* and *Original Sin,* three of the most theological and metaphysical of Edwards's works—understandable, perhaps, given the fact that Miller was the first general editor of the series.

Edwards the intellectual is as multifaceted as Edwards the historical figure. Though emphasized less perhaps by recent than by earlier biographers, his observations of the immediate natural world were penetrating and acute. He describes, as an adolescent "natural philosopher," how woodland spiders "fly" by floating or "swimming" through the air as they change the length of their filament, and notices how one can see their webs at a great distance if the sun is behind them—an optical effect that he understood from reading Isaac Newton on "the incurvation of the rays passing by the edge of any body." He applied Newtonian optics in studying rainbows and the color spectrum, and pondered many curious puzzles—why fire needs air, why bubbles break, why sunlight is warmer at sea level, why lightning bolts zigzag—that would occupy future scientists.[3] Armed with Lockean theories about human understanding as well as Reformation notions about the influx of saving grace, Edwards studied his parishioners almost microscopically in the aftermath of the revivals in which he was involved in order to understand what actually happens to people seized by religious rapture. Psychologists and social theorists utilized his observations about the nature of religious experience into the twentieth century, revivalists still longer.[4] As Samuel Hopkins wrote in the late eighteenth century, Edwards was proficient in "all the arts and sciences" and had a "taste for natural philosophy" that he cultivated with "justice and accuracy" until his death.[5] In Edwards's sermons, the phrase "I have noticed. . ." is a steady refrain.

Edwards's reading reached well beyond Newton and Locke, as is apparent in Peter J. Thuesen's masterfully edited *Catalogue of Books,* where Edwards kept track of his reading, purchase, and loans of books and periodicals. We see, besides a hundred volumes of Reformed theology, titles by the skeptics George Berkeley and David Hume, whose "corrupt" books he felt it important to know. There are titles by the Earl of Shaftesbury and Francis Hutcheson, proponents of a Whiggish anti-absolutist, anti-priestcraft politics of natural virtue; by Joseph Addison and Archbishop John Tillotson on the conformity of Christianity to natural law and the need for tolerance and mutual respect; by English Dissenter Isaac Watts and the Dutchman Christiaan Huygens on astronomy. More surprising are the novels *Clarissa* and *Pamela,* Samuel Richardson's moralistic path-breaking fiction; poems by Alexander Pope, an Anglo-Catholic exemplar of polished satire; and runs of periodicals such as the Whiggish *Guardian* and Addison and Richard Steele's *Spectator* and *Freeholder,* which contained essays on polite manners and British politics.

Edwards was in fact, despite living at the far edge of the Empire, a full participant in a burgeoning eighteenth-century "republic of letters" that transmitted Enlightenment opinion on the efficacy of human reason throughout Europe and North America. He was, to be sure, Jonathan Edwards, not John Locke. His comfort zone was an "evangelical republic of letters" centered in Scotland, the Low Countries, and evangelical

England and New England.[6] Edwards rarely approached the republic of letters as an end in itself, says Thuesen. He saw it rather "as a means of gaining knowledge that could be reapplied for his own evangelical purposes."[7] But that does not make the breadth and scope, the inventiveness and creativity, of his intellect less impressive. The last entry in his book catalogue, made a few months before he died, was a treatise on geometry by a French Jesuit, which he no doubt read in order to perceive God's design more clearly—but also from intellectual curiosity. In Edwards's day, as has been said, "the entire corpus of natural philosophy [science] was still within the capacities of a single scholar." Edwards was such a scholar.[8]

Edwards's sheer powers of reasoning were formidable, comparable in their tenacity and logic to that of the early modern European philosophers, though commonly deployed, since he was a minister and theologian, to defend a position rather than discover one. Exploring the nature of "true virtue," for example, he reasoned as follows from the first cardinal principle of God's greatness: Virtue must consist of "love to God; the Being of beings, infinitely the greatest and best of beings. . . . The *first* objective ground of that love, wherein true virtue consists, is Being, simply considered: and as a necessary consequence of this, that being who has the most of being, or the greatest share of universal existence, has proportionately the greatest share of virtuous behavior, so far as such a being is exhibited to our faculties." Love rooted in this recognition of God's infinite greatness must result not only in due respect and reverence to God but a general public benevolence rather than a love that is "selfish, contracted, narrow." Readers will note the oblique reference to Lockean epistemology and also Edwards's intent to link morality as well as divinity to his near-pantheistic ontology, his definition of all being as, in essence, God. This conception highlights Edwards's "God-entranced" perspective, a product of Puritan doctrine and his own conversion experience that aligns him with similarly God-entranced figures such as Calvin and Augustine. Edwards never questioned the first principle of God's greatness, which left him free to reason from this given and to insist that reason is "the noblest faculty." What he did with it attests to his doggedness as well as his intellectual capacity.[9]

Notwithstanding all this, Edwards still believed that it was necessary to study "what reason *and* Scripture declare," that theologians and ministers need to study the "book of nature" *and* the "book of Scripture." He was fascinated by the "new learning of his day" but was nonetheless "bound by an unparalleled commitment of fidelity to the Scripture."[10] He was in fact a gifted "biblicist," adept at centering a text in a complex scriptural narrative and with an "uncanny" ability to "improve" (in Puritan sermon terminology) a particular doctrine with clusters of citations. In one sermon of 150 manuscript pages, he adduced, literally or in paraphrase, nearly seven biblical texts per page, a "rich mosaic," says M. X. Lesser, of a thousand passages of Scripture for a single sermon.[11] He could reconcile crucial but seemingly conflicting texts—James on justification through works versus Paul on justification through faith. He frequently subjected biblical passages to linguistic analysis, as with a text from Romans on justification or Exodus on hypocrisy, noting how different translations of the Greek or varying historical contexts (legal, poetical, spiritual) could modify surface meanings.[12]

Typology, a common New England way of reading Old Testament references as signposts to the New Testament, served him well, as it served his forebears and contemporaries.[13] Edwards could deploy not merely the poetical and historical voices of, say, Ecclesiastes, Psalms, Proverbs, or the Song of Solomon, but the record of the ancient Hebrews and their prophets, as when he argued that Old Testament imagery prefigured Christ's death and resurrection as acts of self-sacrifice and love; that Jonah and the great fish prefigured the entombment; that Zachariah's "two golden pipes" meant the church of God as found in Matthew, Timothy, and Revelation; that God's very act of creation in Genesis was "a type" of Christ's resurrection.[14] His important disquisitions on the Apocalypse, which informed his understanding of the contours of world history and indeed the very meaning of the creation of the world and the birth, life, and death of Christ, derived from natural phenomena and history, including current events, but heavily and chiefly from Scripture.[15]

As secular scholarly interest in Edwards has begun of late to give way to evangelical and theological interests, this almost photographic memory for Scripture has received greater attention. Yet it may remain Edwards's vigor in incorporating scientific discoveries into the structure of Puritan faith that partly sustains his intellectual reputation—his awareness of Lockean sensationalist psychology as he preached; his argument (adapting Locke) that the human mind has an innate, therefore necessarily

God-given, capacity to shape sensations into meaningful patterns as well
as (contradicting Locke) a sensibility that permits knowledge of the influx of grace; his explanation, after Newton's descriptions of a constantly
moving cosmos held together by gravity, that gravity is none other than
God in action and that God indeed recreates the cosmos moment by moment so that alpha and omega conjoin. In the words of George Marsden,
his latest and finest biographer, Edwards "challenges the commonsense
view of our culture that the material world is the 'real' world." Marsden
calls Edwards's effort to reconcile Augustinian themes with a post-New-
tonian universe "breathtaking."[16] It may be thought to require a kind
of typological thinking to stretch Edwards into the realm of Einstein,
Planck, and Heisenberg in the way Marsden suggests. But the result is
majestic and magical.

Edwards was also a Calvinist, the "last Puritan," struggling heroically
to uphold the principles of the faith of the Reformation thinkers. On
this there is no great disagreement. He was, say scholars, the "greatest of
American Calvinists," a true "Calvinistic thinker," a major force in re-
turning New England to "the essence of the Calvinist faith of its fathers,"
a defender of "Reformed Christianity" and "orthodox Calvinism."[17] At
one point Edwards claimed that he was not a disciple of Calvin, which a
perusal of the *Institutes* makes fairly clear. But he was surely "Calvinistic,"
and it was to preserve and protect the fundamental, and fundamentally
intertwined, elements of Calvinist doctrine in its Puritan guise—God's
omnipotence, original sin, Christ's atonement, the primacy of Scripture,
unearned free grace, sanctification—that Edwards labored to reconcile
traditional Protestantism with Enlightenment thought and social need.
It may indeed be argued that Jonathan Edwards's creed was the chief
source of his immense creative energy, driving him to defend Calvinist
tenets, over hundreds of pages of sermons and treatises, against its adversaries. Without the spur of combat with the anti-Calvinists—Edwards
was nothing if not verbally combative, a trait that ran strongly in Puritan
ranks—he might have written less and be remembered little except for his
sermons and notebooks.

Central to Edwards's faith, its cornerstone and key, was his belief in
an all-powerful, all-knowing, omnipresent God. During his youthful

conversion experience, as he later recalled, he became aware of his "vile self-exaltation," his "universal, exceeding dependence on God's grace and strength," and his delight in the "absolute sovereignty of God." Faith "abases men," he wrote, "and exalts God."[18] He believed in "the absolute priority of deity," says Clyde Holbrook, "the complete dependence of men upon God, God's own glory as the aim of all creation and of man's highest end." Few men, even among the Puritan divines, ever believed in God with more thoroughness and ardor.[19]

Edwards's vision of God and his rhetoric on God could reach sublime heights. God was "infinitely the greatest being," infinitely "beautiful and excellent," infinitely "valuable," the head of the "universal system" of existence, the source of "diffused beams of brightness and glory" throughout the whole of creation.[20] God "hath built the universe," and his sovereignty over it is boundless.[21] And as the universe is ever in motion, God must hold it together, must give it direction and substance through his will, and must sustain it by means of constant creation. What seems material is but God in action. Because God creates the universe anew moment by moment, what seems past thus folds constantly back into present and future. This was a faith "relentlessly" God-centered, a faith, like Augustine's and Calvin's, that was "God-intoxicated."[22] Edwards, maintains Douglas Elwood, was a man "of one idea, and that one idea was God."[23]

Edwards was a Reformation Christian in other ways as well. He believed that the Bible, though susceptible of interpretation, was the revealed and unchanging word of God. He therefore believed in a glorious Heaven and also in a hell of great suffering, and that all people bear the original sin of Adam and Eve and, absent salvation through the unearned and unwarranted free grace of God, are doomed by God, our ultimate judge, to everlasting torment. Humans cannot accomplish their own salvation. God alone grants salvation as he chooses. And the Day of Judgment—the Apocalypse—can come at any moment. Edwards also adhered to the Scriptural account of the birth and life of Jesus Christ, the son of God, a manifestation and incarnation of God himself, a "Man-God" who willingly, lovingly sacrificed himself on the cross to atone for humanity's sins and who offers, for those who believe in him, a path to Heaven instead of perdition. Edwards preaches often on the three "increated" figures of the Trinity, acknowledging its "puzzling mysteries" but also explaining why Christ and not God or the Holy Spirit is "suitable for a redeemer." It is not "meet" that God, who holds the "rights of the Godhead and so [is] the person offended" by humanity, should be Mediator; nor the Holy Spirit, which "already seeks the blessing of God" for humanity. It must be a "middle person," hence Christ, who is simultaneously and inevitably God himself acting at one remove. The Spirit meanwhile helps God's ministers to awaken and revive their flocks and advance the march to the Millennium and the Apocalypse by spreading the Gospel.[24]

Edwards is also Reformed in his attitude toward the Roman Catholic Church, the Antichrist, the "generation of vipers," the "dragon" and "beast" of Revelation.[25] Some of this is mere reflexive Protestantism, including contempt for the "superstitious" belief in, for example, transubstantiation and various dietary restrictions. Some, however, stems from crucial points of dogma—the Protestant insistence on direct access to Scripture, hostility to priestly hierarchy and intercession, and especially antipathy to the practice of selling indulgences. Roman Catholic priests "pretend to sell" precious things that actually belong to the Holy Spirit: "Baptism, regeneration, and salvation; . . . forgiveness of sins, and sanctification in confirmation, and the Eucharist, and ordination, consecration, and extreme unction." All this had become at the time of Luther a "great commodity" for Catholic "merchandise," an extreme and perverted version of the doctrine of justification by works instead of grace, of justification by individual men instead of God. This was anathema to Calvinists, and Edwards attacked Roman Catholicism on these grounds his whole life.[26]

Another doctrine was at stake, too. Edwards longs for the day when Europe, the "house of Antichrist," will come into "the possession of Protestants" because the fall of the papacy would signal the imminence of the Millennium and the Second Coming of Christ, the consummation of human history and God's final sorting of souls for Heaven or hell—"the accomplishment of the church's glory, joy, and laughter after the destruction of Antichrist, or the Church of Rome, that is spiritually called Sodom."[27] It is therefore necessary, in the eighteenth century, to focus not just on the Vatican, the house of the popes of the "seven heads and ten horns," but also on absolutist France, the great Roman Catholic power of the age.[28] Edwards's library contained works, many by Huguenots, detailing French iniquities: Jacobite plots to restore Catholic rule and overturn

British constitutional liberty, recurring military assaults on the British and their colonies, missionary competition among the heathens. He supported from the pulpit his "country," Britain, against the Bourbons and their Indian allies, and combed current events for signs that the French army and all the other minions of the papal Antichrist, including the loathsome Jacobites, might be defeated. If France, the "grand fountain of popery," was "but reformed," then "Antichristendom" would become a "miserable, dry, parched, withered, barren wilderness." When an English Nonconformist predicted that Rome would collapse sometime around the year 2000, Edwards, who more than once thought he discerned the onset of the evangelical age leading to the Millennium, only reluctantly accepted that date. Surely it would not be so long coming.[29]

Edwards, one of the great polemicists of a polemical age, took on all adversaries. He argues, against Hobbes and other materialists, that what seems to be matter is actually God's presence as perceived by human minds. "Nothing has any existence anywhere else but in consciousness," God's as well as man's, "infinite or finite."[30] He argues, against deists who see the universe as God-created but governed by natural law rather than miraculous intervention, that God not only intervenes but is the directing and binding energy of the universe; against proto-Unitarians who deny the Trinity, that the resurrection and ascension show otherwise; against proto-Universalists who think all humanity will be saved, that sin manifestly exists and requires a just God's punishment; against annihilationists who speculate that sinful souls will simply vanish while the saints enjoy Heaven, that sinfulness is "offensive" to God and deserves punishment beyond mere annihilation.[31] He argues, against Arminians who suggest that individuals can achieve their own regeneration through moral training and religious teaching, that they cannot because God is omnipotent and therefore will bestow grace as he will; and against individualists who press the case for individual free will in seeking grace, that people have inherent inclinations toward grace that they may exercise or not, but that God is the only architect of salvation.[32] To argue otherwise, as sophisticated Anglicans and Congregationalists were doing, verges on Roman Catholicism.[33]

The concept of original sin, for Edwards as for all rigorous Calvinists, led to the damnation of unsaved helpless humanity, including helpless infants and children. This was evidently a somewhat unsavory prospect even for Edwards, who tried to soften the effect by preaching that God is loving and merciful. It is God, after all, who proffers the blessing of grace to sinful humanity, in certain instances even to infants according to their "inclination." One calculation was that God grants grace to one percent of infants—better, one supposes, than nothing, and the percentage might anyway be subject to upward revision.[34] He also made curious demographic calculations late in life showing that the population of the earth would multiply so rapidly that virtually all the humanity that had ever lived would be alive at the time of the Millennium. Since the approach of the Millennium would witness widespread regeneration—the best way to predict its coming—most people, all but one in a thousand, would in fact go to Heaven. A nineteenth-century minister, using Edwards's numbers, calculated the ratio as one damned for every 17,000 saved—reassuring odds, one would think. Infants remained a puzzle, though here too there was some give, and there would undoubtedly have been more as Britain and America moved into the child-oriented nineteenth century.[35]

Even modified, wholesale damnation seemed to many a monstrous doctrine that cast God as a callous tyrant. This objection predated Edwards. Thus Lord Herbert of Cherbury, a seventeenth-century deist: "How could I believe that a just God could take pleasure in the eternal punishment of those to whom he had never afforded a method of salvation, and possibly whom he necessarily foresaw as being damned absolutely, with no possibility of escape?"[36] The objection was even more common in Edwards's lifetime. Thus Daniel Whitby, an eighteenth-century English latitudinarian: "To say God seriously invites, exhorts, and requires all Men to work out their Salvation, and yet by his Decree of Reprobation hath rendered that Even to the most of them impossible . . . is to make the Gospel of Christ a Mockery."[37] Rigorous Calvinism was a view ill fitted to those seeking a God of motherly compassion and warmth, and it flew in the face of the Atlantic world's growing trust in reason and individualism. Edwards did not do much to modify it.[38]

Edwards's theology, says Patricia Tracy, was "the Western world's last emphatic statement of man's utter depravity."[39] William Breitenbach calls Edwards "the most imposing apologist for Calvinism and human depravity in United States intellectual history."[40] Both these remarks are seriously overblown, but they do capture something of how he was and is perceived.

This in any case long darkened his reputation. Oliver Wendell Holmes called Edwards's faith "barbaric, mechanical, materialistic, pessimistic." Carl Van Doren called it an "appalling . . . High Calvinism." It was a sign, for the atheist Mark Twain as for the Christian Henry Ward Beecher, of a "resplendent intellect gone mad."[41] Edwards worked through an "outworn dogmatic system," says the generally sympathetic Ola Winslow. He quibbled and attacked when his "whole theological system needed to be demolished." He sometimes laid aside his sectarian theology, she acknowledges. "It is a pity he did not do it more."[42] Despite laudable and well-placed efforts at redress, that reputation, whatever its actual merit, persists.

Yet it may be neither severe Calvinism nor lofty intellectualism that has stamped Jonathan Edwards most deeply for some. It is rather his role in fomenting, furthering, and defending revivalism, including both the Connecticut Valley Revival of the 1730s and the Great Awakening, the outpouring of religious enthusiasm that traversed the British colonies and became one model for the intense emotionalism that would characterize much of later American Protestantism. In particular, it is the "hellfire" sermons that Edwards employed, his tactic of preaching the "terror" of hell to induce spiritual revival, that at the time and historically has largely defined him, making him at best a "pivotal figure in the emergence of international evangelicalism," at worst a "violent and sarcastic preacher of the immediacy of hell-fire," the progenitor, for Samuel Eliot Morison among others, of an anti-intellectual "hot gospeling" that burdened the souls of youth.[43]

The Connecticut Valley Revival began in late winter 1734 in Northampton when Edwards, concerned as usual with the spiritual apathy and worldly behavior of his community, particularly its young people, preached sermons on "sinful mirth" as "ruinous," God's sovereignty "in the work of conversion" and "wrath" against unbelievers, and the "great sin" of resisting "the spirit of God."[44] According to Edwards's 1737 account, young people responded first and then were followed by their elders. "Frolics" and tavern-keeping declined, to be replaced in part by meetings in the minister's house. Church membership and attendance were higher, prayer and charity more visible. "All other talk but about spiritual and eternal things was soon thrown by," writes Edwards. "All the conversation, in all companies and upon all occasion, was upon these things only, unless so much as was necessary for people carrying on their ordinary secular business. . . . People had soon done with their old quarrels, backbitings and intermeddling with other men's matters. . . . Our public assemblies were then beautiful: the congregation was alive in God's service, everyone earnestly intent on the public worship, every hearer eager to drink in the words of the minister as they came from his mouth."[45]

Revivals, or "awakenings," were not altogether novel. Solomon Stoddard had presided over several "awakenings," but these did not reach beyond Northampton and evoked no startling expressions of piety and zeal, which a social conservative such as Stoddard would in any case have disliked.[46] The 1734 Revival, by contrast, spread to dozens of towns and villages throughout the immediate area, and there were a number of conversion experiences of remarkable intensity and great emotional expression, including that of a dying young woman and a four-year-old girl who experienced an ecstatic conversion and proceeded to hector her family about the need for humility and charity. Thrilled at the initial results, Edwards sought to generate additional conversions of this kind by means of preaching that relied not only on reasoned argument and exposition but also on the arousal of strong feelings or "affections" (in Edwardsian terminology)—on preaching to the "heart" as well as the "head"—and that alternated visions of "saintly happiness" with the hellish "wrath of God."[47]

Not all responses to this kind of preaching were positive, most especially that of Edwards's uncle, Joseph Hawley, an industrious landowner and merchant who became so overwrought by anxiety over his unworthiness that he cut his own throat. Hawley's suicide shook Edwards, as did the community's gradual relapse into spiritual "deadness." This and other developments—an outbreak of diphtheria, harsh weather, a captious "party spirit"—seem to have deflated Edwards for the moment. "The Spirit of God was gradually withdrawing from us," to be replaced by "the Devil."[48] By summer's end the Valley Revival was over.

But Edwards did not relinquish the fight or abandon his methods. He continued to preach hard-hitting sermons and completed and published *A Faithful Narrative* of the Northampton experience. Both the experience and the *Narrative* won much praise, including in England. For Isaac

Watts, who wrote an introduction to the first edition, the Valley Revival was "so strange and surprising . . . that we have not heard anything like it since the Reformation." John Wesley himself "read the truly surprising narrative of the conversions lately wrought in and about the town of Northampton, in New England." Surely "this is the Lord's doing and it is marvellous in our eyes."[49] Wesley was soon imitating Edwards's methods and eventually acknowledged him as a fountainhead of revivalism.[50]

There were signs, moreover, as early as late 1739 that the Holy Spirit was again touching hearts, and not just in the Connecticut Valley. In 1740 revivals were emerging in many places. The arrival of George Whitefield, one of the mighty evangelists of the age, helped fuel them, as did the labors of the stentorious Tennent brothers of Pennsylvania and the rise of young "New Light" ministers influenced by Whitefield and Edwards. Edwards played his part—welcoming Whitefield to his pulpit and weeping with him during service, consulting with the Tennents, encouraging students in the use of his methods, preaching to his and other flocks, always observing, ever observing.[51]

He also preached his immortal masterpiece of hellfire terror, "Sinners in the Hands of an Angry God." Solomon Stoddard had insisted that preparation for salvation had to include such preaching ("Men need to be terrified"), and Edwards himself had previously preached on similar themes just as his father had.[52] But "Sinners" rises to new heights in its emphasis on human helplessness, God's capacity to punish, and the unbelievable torments of a fiery hell, an accomplishment that Edwards achieves through the employment of vivid metaphors to express a wrath of God that might send the unregenerate tumbling into a pit, an oven, a mouth, a furnace, flames, a troubled sea, waters dammed by a floodgate or imperiling them by swords, serpents, axes, and arrows about to be "made drunk with your blood." In this sermon Edwards concentrates all his effort on the goal of moving beyond reason to feeling, of making people know, as he said elsewhere, the "sweetness of honey" experientially rather than by mere explanation—except that "Sinners" brought the experience not of sweetness but of unmitigated pain.[53]

The response was stunning: "Great moaning & crying out throughout the whole House—what shall I do to be Saved—oh I am going to Hell . . . shrieks and cries . . . piercing & Amazing . . . Souls were hopefully—

wrought upon." It is the most effective imprecatory sermon in American literature.[54] Isaac Watts, who printed it in Britain and approved of it, nonetheless called it "a most terrible sermon, which should have had a word of Gospel at the end of it." Edwards defended "terror" preaching on the grounds of Scripture, which offers examples of it; on the grounds of psychology, which involves loves, hates, fears, and longings that require stimulation; and on the grounds of man's depravity, which people need to feel as well as know. And even though some modern admirers of Edwards consider "Sinners" to be "infamous," it became much beloved of generations of hellfire revivalists who used facsimiles of it to terrify the guilt-ridden into getting right with God.[55]

Yet the Great Awakening, like its Connecticut Valley precursor, burned itself out, leaving New Englanders little more pious in thought or Christian in behavior than before. It left, moreover, unanticipated problems in its wake. Some were doctrinal. Edwards, like Solomon Stoddard before him, was a "preparationist," meaning that pastors should somehow "prepare" people for grace, if not produce it.[56] The Awakening, however, highlighted the ongoing tension between the belief in God's absolute power, which implied predestination, and the intent to help parishioners feel the Spirit, which implied free will. Later evangelicals handled the tension by the rank expedient of preaching earned grace—that is, free will. Edwards never quite acknowledged that he himself did so.[57] There may have been, too, a sense that revivalism privileged the Holy Spirit over faith in Christ and thus denied the true balance of the Trinity as set out by, for instance, Edwards himself.[58]

And revivalism seemed to elevate emotion (feeling the Spirit) over reason (studying God) or Scripture (believing in Christ), a position that could be construed as non-Puritan, if not non-Christian. "The plain truth," said "Old Light" Boston minister Charles Chauncy in the accents of the Enlightenment, is that "an *enlightened mind,* and not *raised affections,* ought always to be the guide of those who call themselves men; and this, in the affairs of religion, as well as other things." This was powerful criticism even to Edwards, who preached scripture *and* reason, referred to reason as the "noblest or highest faculty," and was a convinced "strict cessationist" who rejected the possibility of new revelation of any kind except that which had occurred in the days of the apostles.[59] Moreover, as he acknowledges, "Nothing so puffs men up as enthusiasm, with a high conceit of their wisdom, holiness, eminency and sufficiency, and makes them so bold, forward, assuming, and arrogant."[60]

The matter of "revelation" was exceedingly pertinent, in fact, to disturbing behavioral issues of the Awakening. In some places parishioners, including young children, were not only moaning and shrieking but collapsing, licking the floor, contorting their bodies, falling into trances, speaking in tongues, voicing direct messages from Christ, dancing in circles all night, and seizing ministers in a fit of hugs and kisses. Radical New Light ministers themselves appeared to incite such behavior by claiming direct inspiration, flailing listeners into a state of "possession," and exhorting them to burn their clothing and other symbols of "idolatry." At least one, James Davenport, seemed mad in the manner of Savonarola. Some, moreover, were itinerants, even lay exhorters, who not only conducted revivals in settled parishes but condemned settled ministers and fomented schism. This kind of disrespect was anathema to the New England churches, and it confirmed Old Lights such as Chauncy in their opposition to the Awakening itself. " 'Tis scarcely imaginable," Chauncy writes, "what excesses and extravagancies people were running into, and even encouraged in." At its extremes revivalism appeared an effusion of the dreaded Antinomian pretensions and anarchy of Anne Hutchinson and James Fox that New England had thought long buried. Unwilling to relinquish a powerful tool for touching men's hearts and fearing to see revivalism in ruins, which would (he thought) unchain individual selfishness and impede progress toward the Millennium and the Apocalypse, Edwards, besides blaming New Light excesses on the Devil, reiterated his commitment to head as well as heart and to holy community as well as gracious individuals. And he labored, in *A Treatise concerning Religious Affections* (preached in 1743, published in 1746), to explain and defend preaching that aroused powerful feelings while providing a set of guidelines to determine whether the Spirit was truly active in souls. *Religious Affections* would eventually join *A Faithful Narrative* and other tracts as a sourcebook for nineteenth-century evangelicals. But for the next few decades, Chauncy and the Old Lights prevailed.

Would Edwards have re-channeled evangelism had he lived longer? Possibly. He continued to cherish the central role of study and reason in faith, and he was in the end deeply critical of enthusiastic excess. *"Let us not despise human learning"* and the "improvement of common knowledge by human and outward means," he writes even as he defends the Awakening.[61] He was also committed to using revival techniques to create loving and holy community, which many successors were not. The following chapters will suggest that he did more than is generally appreciated to refine and channel religious excitement. Yet revivalism's reputation—"distasteful," "incomprehensible," even "grotesque" for many, forever redolent of ill-educated frontiersmen, cynical manipulation, and crude denominational competition whatever its hypothetical merits—clings still to the image of its great progenitor.

Jonathan Edwards was also, for want of a better word, a scold, a persona that plunges us squarely into the middle of colonial Northampton and Puritan New England. A primary duty of a Calvinist minister was not only to prepare individuals for grace but also to correct the sinful ways of his congregation as a whole. Parishioners knew about covenant theology, a notion from the seventeenth century in which God had made a covenant with the Puritans, as he had with the ancient Israelites, that offered favor if they in turn strived to become "cities on a hill"—models of divine grace and holy behavior that would please God and inspire others. John Winthrop articulated this ideal in his famous sermon aboard the *Arbella* at the dawn of the Puritan migration.[62] Over time, as congregations of unregenerate folk inevitably failed to meet this standard, ministers increasingly employed scolding "jeremiad" sermons as a way to castigate their wayward flocks for bringing divine punishments on themselves—epidemics, enemy attacks, and the like.[63]

Parishioners came to expect ministers to criticize them collectively and generally assumed it to be a central element of ministerial duty, all the more since community well-being might depend on sustained efforts to fulfill the covenant. Ministers agreed, including the Hampshire Association of Ministers in discussing a disciplinary matter: "What is the Duty of ministers [toward] any Under their Jurisdiction and Government . . .? Ans. They ought to look upon them as Guilty of contemning Christ's authority, and to deal with them accordingly. (Voted in the affirmative.)"[64]

Edwards, with his belief in original sin, high standards of piety and propriety, and willingness to invoke the threat of punishment, seldom disappointed. In 1727 not long after his ordination in Northampton, he ascribes the tremors of a recent region-wide earthquake to God judging a "corrupt" people and warns of still greater judgments if sins went unrepented and communities unreformed: "Though earthquakes and signs in the Heavens may often have natural causes," they may be "forerunners of great changes and threatenings of judgments" unless a method be found to renew the land and purge it of evil. Else God will "pour out his wrath," as at the time of the "general deluge" in the book of Noah. He might exercise "vindictive" judgments against communities that continue to return to iniquity "as a dog to his vomit" or a sow "wallowing in the mire"—vivid similes for farmers. God could in fact be "more strict in punishing a wicked people in this world than a wicked person." Therefore avoid "works of darkness," or risk "the vengeance of eternal fire."[65]

In an election day sermon in 1730 on "The Dangers of Decline," Edwards calls the whole of Massachusetts Bay to task for forfeiting the "privileges of this land" through spiritual apathy, preoccupation with profit, engagement in business fraud, and political contentiousness. God sometimes allows a people to bring "ruin upon themselves," as after the civil wars of ancient Rome. So beware. The only security from disasters of this kind is to rediscover love by seeking the Spirit in prayer.[66] The titles of Edwards's sermons suggest his recurring theme: "Sin and Wickedness Bring Calamity and Misery on a People," "Bringing the Ark to Zion a Second Time," "Rebellion in Israel."[67]

Scolding of this kind was habitual with Edwards, who seldom preached without at least a few lines chastising his flock, which was after all sinful however divinely blessed. Young people take liberties that seem "sufficient evidences of a prostitute."[68] "No town in America" is so like a "city set on a hill" as Northampton, but it now lies "bleeding amongst us," pierced by selfishness and strife for which God is likely to "spit in our faces" and exercise "awful rebukes while you are eagerly feasting your lusts." He accuses the individual parishioner of being a Pharisee, all "hypocrisy," a "little, wretched, despicable creature; a worm . . . a vile insect."[69] The Edwardsian vocabulary of community chastisement is the lashing of a whip, as in this sampling from 1737 and 1738 alone: hypocrisy, contentiousness, obstinacy, profanity, false doctrine, pride, vanity, declension, covetousness, infidelity, apostasy, and worldliness as well as, of course, worm, dust, insect, and nothing.[70]

In 1737 Northampton built a larger, sturdier meeting house, the location, cost, and interior arrangements of which prompted heated disagreement. Church officers had assigned seats in the earlier structure on benches facing the pulpit according to age, estate, and "usefulness"—community service, military rank, and the like. The planning committee of the new structure took as its task to determine who should be "elevated" and who "degraded."[71] The new building was built with enclosed family pews that were assigned principally by wealth. In the words of Patricia Tracy, the foremost historian of Edwards's pastorate, this implied that property was "more respectable than old age" and worldly achievement "more laudable than experience as a humble Christian."[72]

Edwards objected to this new dispensation. He objected partly because he had been excluded from the formal planning and, unlike the old bench system, the pews allowed some people to sit with their backs to the pulpit—meaning that the minister would no longer be the sole focus of the service. And he objected to the contentiousness of the project and to the arrogance and pride that underlay the seating plan, confirmation that the spirit of the Revival had indeed fled Northampton. Invoking death and God's judgment as great levelers, he warns the congregation, "Consider it is but a very little while before it will be all one to you whether you have sat high or low here."[73]

In the early 1740s Edwards quarreled with the town about arrears in his salary. Only after bitter debate did the taxpayers agree to settle and fix the salary according to certain commodity prices. New England towns paid their ministers well in spite of the undeveloped state of the economy and the chronic fluctuations in the price of agricultural products and land, and Edwards was one of the better paid.[74] But he may have felt a legitimate need for more income. He had no substantial inheritance; his father, who ministered in Connecticut, seems to have scraped by. He had a large family and put up many visitors who rode into Northampton to converse with one of the colonies' best-known revivalists and theologians. He also bought perhaps more than might have been appropriate for, or at any rate good for the reputation of, a farm town pastor—most importantly books whenever and wherever he could but also an occasional present for his wife, a beaver hat and shoe buckles from Boston, education for his children, and a slave or two to work with his several servants. He furthermore believed, as in the meeting house dispute, that the minister should have elevated status in any community calling itself Christian, that it was "anti-ministerial" and therefore "anti-spiritual" to withhold salary, and that this kind of tightfistedness would antagonize God and jeopardize the community's well-being and prospects for grace. And he naturally said so.[75]

In 1744 in the dim afterglow of the Great Awakening, some girls in town told Edwards that young men had been reading a midwifery book, joking about the explicit descriptions and diagrams, and taunting the girls for being "nasty creatures." Long concerned about the potential waywardness of youth, about "night frolics and lascivious behavior" and the untoward use of Sabbath evenings as times for unseemly concourse, Edwards now preached against this instance of "lewd" sinfulness. He then read the names of the miscreants publicly from the pulpit and admonished their families for neglecting their parental duty, an issue he had preached about before. At a meeting in his study, three of the perpetrators openly resisted his, and therefore the church's, authority. One said he would not "worship a wig" and cared not a "turd" or a "fart" for the church's leaders, a clear instance of resistance to conventional notions of patriarchal, and in this case ministerial, prerogative.

Edwards had preached from his earliest days that young people, the future of the community, were in as great peril from Satan as any other group and had much to gain from a loving Christian relationship with God and one another. Faced with this disagreeable Bad Book affair, he naturally expended time and energy scolding such "corruption" and disrespect.[76] In these and other cases the community was reflecting to some degree American trends that would inevitably affect the status and position of local ministers—commercialization in the pew controversy, youth beyond parental control in the Bad Book episode, creeping secularism in the salary squabble. Some ministers bowed to changing circumstances and modified their expectations. Edwards saw the new trends as expressions of impiety, disrespect, selfishness, materialism, arrogance, and other associated collective ills and refused to bend.

In 1742 he went so far as to codify his expectations in a "Northampton Covenant" that pledged signatories to deal honestly in business, come meekly to Christ and his ministerial representative, and eschew avarice and impropriety. Many signed the covenant. Few adhered to its strictures. In the end, with pastor-parish antagonisms high, Edwards, impatient with his unspiritual and uncharitable flock, raised the bar to communion and baptism by requiring a profession of heartfelt faith that incorporated evidence of sanctified behavior. This overturned Solomon Stoddard's ancient permissive practice of free and open communion. In 1750 Edwards was dismissed.[77]

Edwards the scold is evident in the language of the biographers—"harsh disciplinarian," prone to "reprove" and to hold church members to their pledges, "dogmatical and unbending," "strict," "tactless" and "rigid," dedicated to "iron" control.[78] This is an inadequate portrait of the real Edwards, but not exactly an incorrect one. Scolds scold. The towering example of Edwards may indeed be one reason for the persistent if partially unwarranted Puritan reputation for finger-wagging "thou-shalt-not" disapproval. It is certainly one reason why political conservatives of the late twentieth and early twenty-first centuries admire him, although they emphasize how he scolded, for example, bad sexual behavior, but not how, and how often, he scolded bad economic behavior, a distorting omission, as later chapters will argue. Ministerial scolding was not uncommon in early New England. For Edwards, it was indispensable, despite objections to its vehemence at the time and later, to his commitment to the creation of a particular type of holy community.

Old habits died hard. In 1754 at the Stockbridge mission out on the Massachusetts frontier, Edwards, though concerned for and protective of his Indian charges, nevertheless stepped forward, as he had for thirty years, in full scolding mode to chastise his hapless flock as "a poor, miserable people" enslaved to sin—drink, idleness, fighting, and bad family discipline.[79]

❊ 3 ❊

TROPES

A figurative or metaphorical use of a word

Why do Christians sing when they are together? The reason is, quite simply, because in singing together it is possible for them to speak and pray the same Word at the same time; in other words, because here they can unite in the Word.

— DIETRICH BONHOEFFER

INTELLECTUAL, Calvinist, revivalist, and scold are identities suggestive of a stern and judgmental individual, which Jonathan Edwards clearly could be when duty demanded, as it so often did given all that was at stake. Words such as "intense," "tactless," "grave," "stiff," "threatening," "disturbing," and above all "serious" run through the biographical studies.[1]

But these same biographers also use softer, less pejorative terms such as "overconfident," "single-minded," and "certain," and Edwards's own contemporaries saw for the most part a less than frightening figure. The powerful "Sinners" sermon filled the congregation with "cheerfulness and pleasantness" as well as shrieks, says a local diarist. Edwards "wept" at a Whitefield sermon, and Whitefield himself describes Edwards as "adorned with a meek and quiet spirit" and Jonathan and Sarah as wonderful examples of "Christian simplicity," a "sweeter couple" than he had ever seen.[2] Samuel Hopkins, who lived in the Edwards household in the early 1740s, wrote that Edwards was "not a man of many words," was "reserved among strangers," and could appear "unsociable." Hopkins attributed this quietness partly to Edwards's lifelong frailty and partly to his work habits, which kept him in his study many hours a day reading, writing, meeting parishioners, and praying, except in good weather when he rode or walked.

Yet among friends, says Hopkins, he was "easy of access," kind and approachable, "open and free." He was a warm and hospitable host to his frequent guests, always (recorded a visiting minister) "very courteous,"

"kind," and "agreeable." Timothy Dwight, a youthful visitor, describes
him as "relaxed" and readily able to enjoy "cheerful and animated con-
versations" and to enter "truly into the feelings and concerns of his children," who would sometimes be with him on journeys by horseback or to
plant trees.[3] Throughout the difficulties leading to his dismissal in 1750,
he showed, says a contemporary, "not the least symptoms of displeasure
in his countenance," appearing rather like a man whose "happiness was
beyond his enemies' reach" and whose treasure was "not only a future but
a present good."[4]

We know Edwards chiefly through his language. The center of his life
was, in George Marsden's words, "his devotion to God expressed with
pen and ink."[5] And here, too, as with his personality, a more rounded,
less angular Edwards emerges, one who is not predominantly a preacher
of imprecatory "awakening" sermons filled with images of fire and pain.
Powerful as these surely were, they constitute only a small portion, perhaps a few dozen, of his thousand sermons.[6] Images of fire were important, as they are in the Bible. But there are other tropes in Edwards's
work—among them especially light, beauty, harmony, and sweetness—
that also deserve our attention.

Light was Edwards's favorite image and metaphor. He was a man of Scripture, and Scripture enshrines the concept of light from the creation of the
world ("Let there be light") to the coming of the Messiah ("I am the light
of the world"). He was also a man of his time. Though Edwards sometimes mocked them, *luminaires* such as Newton (and the early Edwards)
sought "enlightenment" by studying the nature of light and its revelations
and so began to shift human perceptions of the universe. Edwards, who
knew his optics as well as his Bible, employed the concept of light more
frequently, and looked more avidly for its true meaning and carried it to
greater rhetorical heights, than anyone else of his day.[7] "Jesus Christ the
Light of the World" was a poetic early effort. His first major published
sermon was *A Divine and Supernatural Light,* followed shortly by, among
others, "Jesus Christ is the shining forth of the Father's glory," "False
Light and True," and "Light in a Dark World, a Dark Heart." And on to
the very end in Northampton with "Sons of Oil, Heavenly Lights," an
ordination sermon, and in Stockbridge to his Indian charges, "Of Those
Who Walk in the Light of God's Countenance."

Light represents, as is self-evident and imperative for Edwards, first and foremost the beams of God's glory, the "external expression, exhibition and manifestation of the excellency" of God the "luminary," as if it were the "abundant, extensive emanation and communication of the fullness of the sun to innumerable beings that partake of it." These glorious beams of light are "*of* God, and *in* God, and *to* God."[8] The Father, ever the dominant figure of the Trinity, "is as the substance of the sun," bathing the air with light as it "warms, enlivens and comforts the world."[9] It was the light of God that was revealed to Judea and the Jews, making of them a place and people of light in the engulfing ancient darkness.[10] The visions of "light and glory" that John, Peter, and other apostles saw were "an emanation of the glory of God filling the New Jerusalem."[11] Saints even today are blessed to "walk in the light of God's countenance" and witness the "brightness or light of his face" and the shining of his "favor and love." And more than merely seeing, they enjoy a "constant and perpetual dwelling" in this "animating, quickening light of life." They are "children of light" as God is the "Father of Lights." God contains the very "nature of light or wisdom or moral good," with no darkness in him. He is "the Father of *light,* and only of light."[12]

Like most New England ministers, Edwards also understood light as, in Mark Valeri's phrase, a "trope for the Holy Spirit"—the moment of revelation, the saving influx of the Spirit, the active awakening dimension of God that brings light "into a created mind" instead of shining from it.[13] As God is the light of the sun, so the Holy Ghost "is as the action of the sun, which is within the sun . . . and being diffuse, enlightens, warms, enlivens and comforts the world." The Spirit, "God's infinite love to himself and happiness in himself," is how "God communicates himself [as] the emitted beams of the sun."[14] So communicated, it is the "light that gives evangelical humiliation" and readies humanity for grace and vision.[15]

"A mind," Edwards contends, "not spiritually enlightened [by the Bible and the Spirit] beholds spiritual things faintly, like fainting, fading shadows . . . like a man that beholds the trees and things abroad in the night. . . . He has but a little notion of the beauty of the face of the earth." But when "the light" shines upon him, ideas appear with "strength and distinctness; and he has that sense of the beauty of the trees and fields given him in a moment." A man reasoning without "divine light" is like a man who goes in the dark into a garden full of "the most beautiful plants, and most artfully ordered," and feels them and measures their placement. But "he that sees by divine light is like a man that views the garden when the sun shines upon it."[16]

Light stands frequently in Edwards for Christ, the "Man-god" intermediary between God and humanity. The Holy Spirit works on the souls of men, as in the revivals and awakenings, but chiefly as an enabler to reveal Christ as the light of the world and the image of God and the path to salvation. Who could more properly be the "light" showing God's glory than Christ, the great prophet and teacher of mankind, the light of the world and revealer of God to creatures? Christ is the "effulgence" of God's glory, his perfect image.[17] As prophesied in Isaiah, Christ the Messiah will be as "the light of the morning," a "light to the Gentiles."[18] As head of the future church, he is as the "morning sun arising after a night of darkness" or as the "sun breaking" from a cloud.[19]

When the apostles saw Christ at the time of the resurrection, they saw "light in Christ's person," and in his garments that were "white as the light" and appeared as if "lighted up." The glory in the bright cloud above appeared "shining on Christ," thus communicating God's "excellent brightness" from within rather than as a mere reflection of the light of the sun. "All light is sweet," but this was "immensely more sweet than any other."[20] Christ is the "true light," so that New Englanders in darkness must cleave with "full inclination and affection" to the "revelation of Christ as our Savior."[21] And Edwards offers this evocation of sunlight as it awakens the Northampton landscape in imitation of Christ: "As the sun revives the plants and trees and fruits of the earth, so Christ Jesus by his spiritual light revives the soul and causes it to bring forth fruit. In the winter, the trees are stripped of their leaves and stand naked, cease growing and seem to be dead. . . . But when the sun returns, then all things have the appearance of a resurrection [and] the fields, meadows, and woods seem to rejoice."[22]

Light could burn as well as brighten, as the Bible teaches, and Edwards frequently coupled the two for dramatic effect. Christ, he titles a sermon, was a "burning and a shining light." At the Second Coming, the "light and glory" of Christ's appearance "will be intolerable to the wicked; it shall be like the fire of a furnace to their souls," though "pleasant, and joyful, and healthful to the saints."[23] Fire was the source of all light, whether direct or reflected, in the world of the eighteenth century, including that of the sun. Fire was always in a sense implied by light, which could therefore bring both destruction and illumination. Christ's eyes will be "joyful" light to those with grace, yet at the same time be "piercing flames" to the lost. Christ will be a "glorious morning" to the saved, as when "this Sun arises after such a long night, and their souls shall grow and flourish . . . so that they shall grow up as calves of the stall"—but that same sun would be "scorching" to the unregenerate, setting them "a-fire as stubble."[24] The lesson, offered as usual in the agrarian language of both the Connecticut Valley and the lands of the Israelites, is clear. The sun "makes plants to flourish when it shines after rain; otherwise it makes them wither." And so "light and comfort, if the heart is not prepared by humiliation, do but make the heart worse" by filling it with the "disease of pride" and destroying "the welfare of the soul."[25] But for the blessed, light triumphs in the end.

Edwards also contrasts light with its antithesis, darkness: "All [God's] light arises out of darkness."[26] All Heaven's orbs are "glorious, luminous bodies," while the grave is "dark and silent.[27] Those whom God has called into "marvelous light" should be "done with darkness." It "becomes the children of light to abhor the works of darkness." Sinners wander in "worse-than-Egyptian darkness," but when converted they go "out of one region into the other, out of a region of darkness into the land of light." It is "wonderful" that "light should be made to shine into those hearts that are naturally under the power of darkness."[28]

The passing of night into day was a particular Edwards favorite, as in this long and beautiful treatment of the coming of John the Baptist to prophesy Christ: "First the daystar rises; next follows the light of the sun itself, but dimly reflected, in the dawning of the day; but this light increases, and shines more and more, and the stars that served for light during the foregoing night, gradually go out, and their light ceases, as being now needless, till at length the sun rises, and enlightens the world by his own direct light, which increases as he ascends higher above the horizon, till the daystar itself is gradually put out, and disappears."[29] Edwards had other rhetorical uses for light, as for example a curative (following the contrast with darkness) for "opening the eyes of the blind" who would

have "light given them that were totally destitute of it."[30] The play of
light during eclipses of the moon and sun, with their shifting shadows
and reflections, particularly captivated Edwards, who worked this conceit
into many writings.[31]

Light also, despite the importance of the Holy Spirit and the influx of
grace, is emblematic of human reason. It is a "means of instruction and
persuasion," the "knowledge and understanding of a mind," the "plain
reason" permitting "apprehension of the Word of God."[32] Young people's
vain and carnal behavior is "unreasonable," requiring a man to "put out
the lights of his reason" to be able to enjoy it.[33] And light could serve as
a beacon, a defense, and a weapon, as in the pillar of fire for the Israelites
and the sun that foiled the Egyptians.[34] In days of tribulation and trouble
for his people, God provides "light sufficient to guide and direct them"
and will provide, if need be, sufficient "clear light" to destroy "the Antichrist" himself.[35]

"Christ," Edwards promises, "will fight by increasing [the saints'] light,
and so their enemies shall be destroyed."[36] Light is, indeed, so central a
concept for Edwards that he feels constrained to warn against Quaker
interlopers and their false "inner light"—come to Northampton "hoping
to find good waters to fish in"—and, even more urgently, against Satan's
ploy of cloaking himself as an "angel of light."[37] Pure white light could
also break into "beautiful colors," as from the "feathers of a dove" that
symbolize the "graces of the Heavenly dove" or the precious stones of the
ornaments of the temples and gates of the New Jerusalem that "represent
spiritual things."[38]

Nowhere was this more evident than in the rainbow, the subject of
some of Edwards's most memorable writing, and the inspiration for some
of his most interesting youthful scientific observations. A rainbow is God's
token of his gracious covenant with mankind that "encompasses God" on
his throne as with "mercy." The light of the rainbow round God's throne
is predominantly emerald according to Revelation, a "lively and lovely"
and "cheerful" green, the color of "life, flourishing, prosperity, and happiness" and of "joy and gladness," not so "dull as blue or purple, and yet
most easy to the sight" as compared to "fiery" reds and yellows—a fit
emblem, therefore, of divine grace.[39]

The rainbow that follows the rain is light reflected through a multitude of drops that are like "God's jewels," each a "little star" representing the saints in Heaven, the children of Christ receiving and reflecting "the light of the sun just breaking . . . out of the cloud that had been till now darkened." The whole rainbow, "composed of innumerable, shining, beautiful drops, all united in one, ranged in such excellent order, some parts higher and others lower, the different colors, one above another in such exact order," is the church of saints, "each with its peculiar beauty, each drop very beautiful in itself, but the whole as united together much more beautiful."[40]

A completed rainbow would be a perfect circle, "the most perfect figure, in every part united" as in the church of Christ. It would form an image of the "most pleasant and perfect harmony" could we but see it whole from on high like the Apostle John. It would be a veritable "fountain of all light and love." Each drop of a rainbow holds in itself a likeness of the sun, one with a red image, one a yellow, another a green, another a blue, to symbolize the special features of each of the saints and the gradations of saints. Each drop also represents man, "a very small thing, of little value," "mutable and unstable" and needing the light of grace to conjoin into perfection. Each drop holds both fire and water, "the contrary principles that are in the saints, flesh and spirit"—a "bright spark of Heavenly fire" amidst water "yet not quenched," mere water alone with no brightness except through the "beautiful light in them" from the sun, the fire of Heaven.[41]

Ministers, with their dual burden of spreading Christ's message and coaxing the wayward to better behavior, were special objects of Edwards's light preaching, all the more as he encountered difficulties in his own ministry. Some of the results are extraordinary. In an ordination sermon in the nearby hamlet of Pelham in 1744, he exhorts the new minister, a Scottish Presbyterian and fellow New Light preacher, to be "a Burning and a Shining Light"—burning with "ardor" and with the fervor and zeal of the Holy Spirit yet shining with "pure, clear, full doctrine" based in deep knowledge of Scripture.

"When divine light and heat attend each other in ministers of the gospel," preaches Edwards on this occasion, employing his immense metaphorical powers and distinct cadences, "their light will be like the beams of the sun, that don't only convey light, but give life; and converts will

... spring up under their ministry, as the grass and the plants of the
field under the influences of the sun; and the souls of the saints will be
likely to grow, and appear beautiful ... and their light will be the light of
Christ." Ministers, he says, deploying a string of light images, are "a light
to the souls of men, a lamp in God's temple, and a star in the spiritual
world." God, he says to the new Pelham pastor, has brought you here
[from Scotland] to make you "a burning and shining light ... to cause
this wilderness to bud and blossom as the rose ... and to cause you to
shine in the midst of this people with warm and lightsome, quickening
and comforting beams, causing their souls to flourish, rejoice and bear
fruit, like a garden of pleasant fruits, under the beams of the sun." In this
way you will be "the vehicle of the influence and blessings of the Heavenly world which is a world of light and love." You yourself shall not only
shine as the "brightness of the firmament," but shall someday meet your
church members "in glory," where they shall "shine there around you, as
a bright constellation in the highest Heaven."[42]

Wilson Kimnach argues that Edwards transformed the concept and
usage of light during his prime preaching years.[43] The 1744 ordination
sermon helps validate that claim. The sermon was possibly of less consequence than some others to Edwards because he delivered it in Pelham,
a mere miniscule byway of a village. Moreover, he delivered it in the difficult days after the Awakening had faded and town-pulpit tensions were
rising, both of which were sapping Edwards's energy and optimism. Its
power and beauty are therefore all the more remarkable.

Beauty is a trope that bids fair to rival light in Edwards's work. "The
significance of beauty for Edwards," says Roland Delattre, "is difficult to
overstate."[44] Tibor Fabiny says that he "resonated to the sense of beauty"
in a way that is rare for a Protestant.[45] Beauty, synonymous in most of
his work with "excellency" and perfection, was in fact fundamental to his
understanding of God and humanity, and his treatment of the idea marks
the development, according to some scholars, of a more or less novel
religious aesthetic.[46]

What, besides the abstractions of excellence and perfection, did Edwards mean by beauty? He says in a formal way that beauty is the "mutual
consent and agreement" of diverse things with the features of "regularity,

order, uniformity, symmetry, proportion, harmony." Beauty is the "sides of a square, or equilateral triangle, or of a regular polygon" or the parts of a circle or ellipse or sphere.[47] It is things "concatenated" and converging into "beautiful symmetry and proportion."[48] Things are more beautiful if they are complex ("diverse") and properly placed for their purpose ("efficient") than if they are simple and scattered. Negatively, it is the absence of "deformity," i.e., the disruption of proper form. Any sign of "deformity" or "disproportion" diminishes the effect of beauty.[49]

Edwards couples the word beauty nearly always with some other noun or adjective, and if we examine the pairings we find, besides excellence and perfection, beauty and love, beauty and ornament, beauty and holy, beauty and harmony, and sweet, and ravishing, and comely, divine, supreme, lovely, agreeable, charming, cordial, true, spiritual, pleasant. Clyde Holbrook calls Edwards's language "the austere language of symmetry and proportion."[50] Here we may simply note that the language could be fully as poetic as it was austere.

Edwards's appreciation of beauty began with nature as he experienced it in the partially settled Connecticut River valley of the early eighteenth century. As a boy, Edwards recalled, he built secret places of prayer in the woods, where he immersed himself in nature. As an adolescent he found woods and fields, the stars at night, thunderclouds by day, rainbows and flowers all beautiful with "the sort of beauty which is called 'natural,' as of vines, plants, trees, etc." Because of their "complicated harmony [and] proportion, therein is their beauty."[51]

He writes, when a little older, of the "wonderful suitableness of green for the grass and plants, the blue of the sky, the white of the clouds, the colors of flowers," the "gentle motions of trees, of lily, etc.," the great "suitableness between the objects of different senses . . . as between the colors of the woods and flowers, and the smell, and the singing of birds." The fields and woods "seem to rejoice," as they did in his early childhood, "and how joyful do the birds seem to be in it." How much a "resemblance is there of every grace in the fields covered with plants and flowers," and then the sun breaks forth and "shines serenely . . . upon them."[52] The beauty of the "trees, Plants, and flowers with which God has bespangled the face of the Earth is Delightsome, the beautiful frame of the body of Man, especially in its Perfection is Astonishing, the beauty of the moon and stars is wonderfull, the beauty of highest Heavens, is transcendent."[53] Beauty is the purity, sublimity, and glory of the visible Heavens "in a calm and temperate air, when one is made more sensible of the height of them and of the beauty of their color" and how they denote the "blessedness of the Heavenly inhabitants."[54]

And not only is nature beautiful, so are people and their contrivances. The agreement of the colors, figures, dimensions, and distances of the spots on a chess board, Edwards explains, are beautiful, as are the figures on a piece of chintz or brocade and the right proportions of a human countenance or body or of a melodious tune. The beauty of the solar system or a rose affects the mind, but so does the architecture of a church or palace.[55] Trees and clouds are beautiful. So are jewels, honeycombs, structures, fabrics, a bride's clothing, the pleasantness of light or food or floral fragrances, groups of pious young people, a professing community, strong young women, the "cast of an eye," the "smile of [a] countenance."[56]

Some "corporeal" entities, especially those with more "diversity," proportion, order, and symmetry, are more beautiful than others. A "complex" building with an efficient purposeful ensemble of well-designed pillars and floor marbles, or skillful mortis-and-tenon construction, is more excellent in Edwards's view than a simple one without them. There are also beauties that are "palpable and explicable, and there are hidden and secret beauties. The former pleases and we can tell why." The latter sort, such as a humble violet, are those that "delight us and we can't tell why" without knowing "what secret regularity or harmony it is that creates that pleasure." These hidden beauties are "by far the greatest, because the more complex a beauty is," often with unfathomable "millions" of variables, "the more hidden is it."[57] And the more important a thing is to us—a well-proportioned human instead of a violet—the more beautiful it appears.[58]

There is not only corporeal but "immaterial" beauty—a "beauty of order in society," as when King David brought his people "into the most exact and beautiful order," a loveliness in true religion and a well-wrought church and (no surprise considering the writer) in the ideas of philosophers and theologians, particularly those that lead to "*wisdom*" and to the proper exercise of "*justice.*"[59] The immaterial was even more likely to be beautiful than the corporeal: "When we behold the beauties of minds more immediately than now we do the colors of the rainbow, how ravishing will it be!"[60] Beauty is symmetrical and regular. But it is also "pleasant" and "agreeable" and "comely" and "sweet."[61] Why do even men who seem miserable love life? Because, says Edwards in an astonishing and unforgettable sentence, "they cannot bear to lose the sight of such a beautiful and lovely world."[62]

Edwards frequently uses the example of human loveliness in discussing beauty—the "cast of an eye," a well-proportioned figure, "the smile" of a countenance, "a beautiful body, a lovely proportion, a beautiful harmony of features of face, delightful airs of countenance and voice, and sweet motion and gesture." And when we see "beautiful airs of look and gesture, we naturally think the mind that resides within is beautiful." We observe, says Edwards, what love people may have for fellow creatures and how we incline to "the other sex!" God contrives for us to love fellow creatures, especially "the other sex," and the more exalted the mind of that person, the more "laudable" the love.[63]

Edwards seems clearly to have a female person in mind here, and in fact he penned these lines when he was courting Sarah, the girl who would become his wife.[64] He seems to have begun falling in love with Sarah Pierpont at about twenty years old. He wrote, on the fly leaf of a book he later gave her, that she "has a strange sweetness in her mind and sweetness of temper, uncommon purity in her affections. . . . She is of a wonderful sweetness, calmness and universal benevolence; especially after . . . God has manifested himself to her mind." She seems to have "someone invisible always conversing with her."[65]

Sarah, for Edwards, possessed mental as well as physical beauty. If a statue could look the same way, Edwards explains, we should not be "so delighted with it" or fall "entirely in love" with it because we would know it had "no perception or understanding." We look upon "this agreeableness, these airs, to be emanations of perfections of the mind, and immediate effects of internal purity and sweetness," especially when we "love the person" for her "voice, countenance and gesture," which have so much greater power over us than bare "colors and proportion of dimension." There is an analogy, he says, between "such a countenance and such airs" and "these and those excellencies of the mind." This has been the same, he continues, everywhere and for all ages, and it connotes spiritual as well as mental beauty. "Lovers delight so much" in flowers and bespangled meadows because there is an "analogy" between the beauty of the skies, trees, and the like and "spiritual excellencies." The Son of God, thus communicating himself to the world, enables "beauty of face and sweet airs," like flowery meadows and gentle breezes and crystal rivers and the golden edges of the evening cloud, to be shadows of divine excellence.[66]

All versions of beauty, whether corporeal or immaterial, simple or complex, are in fact only secondary beauty, argues Edwards, as they are in nature and in Sarah Edwards. They are shadows and representations of the breathtaking primary beauty of God, suggestive of but inferior to the spiritual beauty that natural objects exemplify but that lie beyond the grasp of natural unregenerate man. Natural beauty is "some image of the true, spiritual original beauty" which, though "surpassing the art of man," is beautiful to the degree it may "shadow forth" spiritual beauty.[67] Beauty exhibits its pleasing features of regularity, similarity, proportion, and so forth because, says Edwards, those are the essential features of God and of Jesus Christ. Beauty is diversity, proportion, symmetry, and order because God has implanted within us an "instinct" to love them as the "image of an higher kind . . . of spiritual beings."[68]

In other words, it has "pleased God" to establish this "law of nature," and he has so constituted the world that "inferior beauty, especially in those kinds of it which have the greatest resemblance of the primary beauty, as the harmony of sounds, and the beauties of nature," enlivens a sense of "spiritual beauty." Perceiving beauty in this way enables us to intuit, if only dimly, the essence of God, the source of all beauty, because nature is full of the "emanations, or shadows, of the excellencies of the Son of God" from whose "efficiency" flow the beauties of the universe.[69]

Without grace, man can discern little of this divine beauty, "any more than a man, without the sense of tasting, can conceive of the sweet taste of honey; or a man without the sense of hearing can conceive of the melody of a tune; or a man born blind can have a notion of the beauty of the rainbow."[70] The beauty of divine holiness evident to the saints is, by contrast, all but beyond expression, though Edwards struggles to express it anyway. "God is God, and distinguished from all other beings, and exalted above 'em, chiefly by his divine beauty."[71] He is "the foundation and

fountain of all being and all beauty," whose excellence, glory, and beauty
are "infinite." He is an "infinite, eternal, and immutable excellency; he
is not only an infinitely excellent being, but a being that is infinite excellency, beauty, and loveliness."[72]

God's holiness is a "most beautiful, lovely thing . . . sweet and ravishingly lovely," the "highest beauty and amiableness, vastly above all other
beauties." It makes the soul "Heavenly and far purer than anything" on
earth. It is of a "sweet, lovely, delightful, serene, calm, and still nature,"
almost "too high a beauty for any creature to be adorned with." It makes
the justified soul "a little, amiable, and delightful image of the blessed Jehovah" that angels may look upon with "pleased, delighted, and charmed
eyes." What a "sweet calmness, what a calm exstacy, doth it bring to the
soul!"[73] The sight of the beauty of divine things, writes Edwards, will
excite "true desires and longings of soul" after those things, "natural free
desires, the desires of appetite; the thirstings of a new nature; as a new-
born babe desires the mother's breast; and as a hungry man longs for
some pleasant food he thinks of; or as the thirsty hart pants after the cool
and clear stream."[74]

There is therefore not only spiritual beauty and external beauty. There
is also God as "beauty within himself, consisting in being's consent with
his own being."[75] God delights in his own excellence and creates the universe as an expression of this divine excellence so that it may be known
and admired. For Edwards, God's goal in his ongoing acts of creation and
recreation is therefore not human happiness but, in the formulation of E.
Brooks Holifield, the "diffusion of his own 'excellent fullness' for its own
sake."[76] The very work of salvation and the exercise of virtue involve the
excellency or the beauty of consent of saints to God because the union
of the regenerate heart to "Being in general," or to "God the Being of beings," is the highest form of beauty or excellency. And Edwards's description of the long Millennial era signaling the approach of the Apocalypse,
a notable part of his theology, glows with the imagery of excellence, as
in his anticipation of "one church, one orderly, regular, beautiful society,
one body, all the members in beautiful proportion."[77]

The appreciation of worldly beauty, says Edwards, is no evidence per se
of true virtue or virtue of the heart or of the essentials of the good society
that we shall explore in this book.[78] Yet a concept that makes beauty a

central ontological and doctrinal concept is relevant to a consideration of
God's presence in humanity, to human social relations, and to Jonathan
Edwards. And it is, per se, beautiful.

Harmony, the handiwork of God and an indisputable element of physical, social, spiritual and divine beauty, was a primary value for Edwards,
as we have seen—integral to excellence, a companion word to beauty,
the concatenation of symmetry and proportion, the natural focus of the
instinct that God has implanted within us to love regularity, similarity,
and order—"the beauty, harmony and order, regular progress, life and
motion, and in short, all the well-being of the whole frame."[79]

Edwards saw harmony in the places we might expect him to, and in a
few places we might not expect. There is a "general harmony of things,"
a "general excellency, that is harmony," as shown through observation
and reason and in Scriptural passages revealing the perfections of the
cosmos.[80] Nature, as "vines, plants, trees, etc.," consists of a "complicated
harmony," as do the "motions and tendencies and figures of bodies" in
the universe."[81] Our senses are so contrived that we notice "the rules of
harmony and regularity" in small matters such as how we walk or hold
our hands when moving about a room or how the "strokes of an acute
penman" have so intelligent an order and relationship that they seem
intrinsic to the strokes themselves.[82] We perceive, by way of "harmonies
of sight and sound," the systematic "regular motion" of animals—birds,
for example, flying "to sing in the firmament."[83] We see people's "countenance, or shape" and "gracefulness of motion," and hear their "harmony
of voice."[84] There is harmony in contrivances such as clocks and other
machines.[85] Harmony is evident even in "marks or spots" on the floor or
wall, which our imagination arranges into "parcels and figures" of "pleasing proportion."[86]

"Spiritual harmonies" are, understandably in Edwards, of "vastly larger
extent" than physical harmonies, with "vastly oftener redoubled" proper-
ties and many more "beings," with one beneficial to another as in "a type
of love or charity in the spiritual world." They therefore require a special
lens to comprehend them; that is, they must be understood typologically
by means of the interpretation of the imagery of nature itself.[87] The glory
of the face of the earth is "grass and green leaves and flowers" which last

awhile "and then are gone," withered after spring and summer by a winter (in New England anyway) that "defaces" the land. The glory of the Heavens, by contrast, the realm of God, continues through both winter and summer, "age after age," never fading just as the "glory and happiness of Heaven" never fade. So, too, a mother bird feeding her nestlings is a picture of harmony emblematic of Christ sheltering his saints like children with the "warmth and heat of the Holy Spirit and the Heavenly Dove."[88] The very "regularity and harmonious order of the world" is how God "manifests his nature and so accomplishes his purposes in creating it."[89]

God's word in Scripture suggests the harmony not only of the cosmos but of social order.[90] At one point Edwards invokes the "harmony of millennial society," that eagerly awaited thousand-year epoch that will precede the Apocalypse and signal its coming and during which "all nations in all parts, on every side of the globe" shall be knit together in "sweet harmony" and enjoy universal peace and love.[91] But he refers, in addition, to the patterns of God's present-day decrees. "God decrees all things harmoniously and in excellent order; one decree harmonizes with another," as in the decree that people must pray for rain and the decree that drought-ending rain must fall. He decrees good preaching, free grace, and true faith in Jesus Christ. He decrees, says Edwards, "diligence and industry" and therefore prosperity, and also "prudence" and therefore success, "good natural faculties" and therefore learning, "summer" and therefore the growing of plants, conformity to Christ and therefore a "calling." He decrees in the end "everlasting glory." Thus "all the decrees of God are harmonious" because they are simultaneous.[92]

One of Edwards's projects was to "harmonize" the Bible by demonstrating (largely through typological readings and the interpretation of prophecies) the unity of the "Genius, Spirit, Doctrine, and Rules of the Old Testament and the New."[93] This was a lifelong ambition; a late unpublished work bore the title "Harmony of the Old and New Testament."[94] One result of these labors was his frequent use of Old Testament texts to demonstrate the role of music and song in inspiring harmonious relations. Exodus and Hosea describe the "joy and songs of the children of Israel at escaping the bondage of Egypt.[95] "Hannah's song" in Samuel refers to "gospel times."[96] Verses in Jeremiah, Isaiah, and other prophetic Old Testament books predict "joyful songs" with the coming of the Messiah, songs heard from the "ends of the earth" that all nations should sing from the heights of the "new Zion" in a new manner. "The mountains and trees of the field, and all creatures, sun, moon and stars, Heaven and earth" will "break forth into singing," and "even the dead should awake and sing," and the tongues of the "dumb" and the "barren, the prisoners, the desolate, and mourners should sing."[97] The Book of Psalms shows us the "songs of Zion," the "sacred" or "Lord's songs" of God's church that were formed by "divine direction" and made crucial to "the very matter of worship."[98]

Edwards had some musical training when young, sang himself, and sang with his family, though not apparently during service in order to save his voice, perhaps a concession to his frailty. Sarah, too, sang, sometimes to herself, as did Edwards's children and grandchildren. All this attuned him to the power of music, "especially sacred music," which has an "efficacy to soften the heart into tenderness, to harmonize the affections," and to give the mind "harmonious exercise" and a "relish for objects of a superior character."[99]

He compares the wonderful vision of the saved to a deaf man hearing music for the first time, and uses the example of music to distinguish between appreciating simple as opposed to complex beauty.[100] Birds, brute creatures, and little children delight in only a few notes. Men and women aware of music's "thousands of different ratios" will apprehend the full sweet harmony of complex music. "The best, most beautiful, and most perfect way" to express a "sweet concord of mind to each other, is by music." The happiest imaginable society is where people "express their love, their joy, and the inward concord and harmony and spiritual beauty" of their souls by "sweetly singing to each other." The regenerate soul, he says, "distinguishes as a musical ear." In Heaven, in fact, the saints will probably express this concord in ways "more proportionate, harmonious and delightful" than mere natural sound, and will make music with "organs" adapted to the purpose in "infinitely more nice, exact and finer proportion" than we can in our "gross air."[101]

It is no surprise, given Edwards's sense of the spiritual value of music, that he was instrumental in shaping the way his community sang. When he assumed the Northampton pastorate, the congregation had already begun to change its service psalmody from the Old Style, where women remained silent while men repeated lined-out verses from the metrical but melody-less Bay Psalm Book unaccompanied by instruments, to a New Style, still based on the Psalms and devoid of instruments but with everyone, including children, trying to sing to a common beat and melody. Old Style traditionalists, led apparently by Presbyterians, argued against such an elitist, imposed, unscriptural, possibly "papist" invasion of tradition, but the New Style swept through the region anyway, becoming especially popular with young people, some of whom enrolled in singing classes taught by itinerant music teachers.[102] Northampton made the transition fairly smoothly, it seems, guided no doubt by the predilection of Solomon Stoddard.

But Edwards wanted more, and in the 1730s he worked to incorporate new features into local singing. One of his inspirations was the English Dissenter Isaac Watts, whose original sacred hymns and paraphrases of the Psalms had not only melody and meter suitable even for children—the Edwards grandchildren memorized some of them—but also choruses and rhymed verses amenable to multi-part harmonies. A New England model was Cotton Mather, who was active in persuading East Coast ministers to incorporate more beautiful, holy, "orderly" harmonies into their worship.[103] By the time of the Northampton revival Edwards could write proudly that his congregation's singing "excelled . . . generally carrying regularly and well three parts of music, and the women a part by themselves." As he organized small prayer and devotional meetings in town to stimulate community affections and revival-generated Christian behavior, he also encouraged parishioners to sing in this lovelier, more joyous, more "harmonious" way and in 1736 argued, in the face of weakening revival fervor, that praise of God in psalms and hymns was now all the more essential. A few years later amidst the excitement of the Great Awakening, the Northampton services on Sunday afternoon began to include the singing of hymns as well as Psalms.[104]

Edwards worked harmony as deeply into the structure of his belief as into the form of his congregation's worship. "All natural operations," he writes, "are done immediately by God only in harmony and proportion," with the "highest kind of operations" possessed of the most general proportion "from eternity to eternity."[105] There is a "wonderful resemblance" and agreement in God's manner of working in nature. And since he "does

purposely make and order one thing to be in an agreeableness and harmony with another," he must by extension do the same in the spiritual
world—an insight that shaped Edwards's enduring sense that the excellence of the divinity consists of harmony, symmetry, and proportion.[106]

But God as an entity also embodies Edwardsian concepts of harmony,
implying not just proportion and regularity but disposition (attitude)
and consent ("consentaniety") as in the "mutual consent and agreement"
of diverse things, a concept he developed at different levels.[107] At the
theological level, says Sang Hyun Lee, God himself is essentially a "relation" of proportion and harmony because God in the guise of the Trinity
of Father, Son, and Holy Spirit is inherently and obviously plural and
therefore necessarily and inevitably relational. Edwards attacked Arians
and incipient Unitarianism on the grounds that God's excellence requires
a harmony of consent, which in turn requires a plural Godhead with the
capacity and disposition to consent within itself.[108] In Edwards's formulation, written when he was only twenty but fundamental to his belief
thereafter, "One alone cannot be excellent. . . . If God is excellent, there
must be a plurality in God, otherwise, there can be no consent in him."
We have, ineluctably, a "harmony of God's Attributes." Moreover, "God
is love," and without a Trinity divine love has no outlet.[109]

The social implications of this view are immense. At the ethical level,
true virtue comprises "consent, propensity and union of heart"—first to
the plurality of the Trinity, secondly to God manifesting himself in the
universe as "Being in general," finally to our fellow humans by means of
grace.[110] A "lively exercise of virtue" occurs when a man sees God as "most
congruous and harmonious."[111] "Consent of being to being" in this manner is the essence of all love.[112] For Edwards, summarizes Herbert Richardson, virtue is love for all things in their "universal harmony."[113]

At the level of the moment of the influx of grace, Edwards employs
the language of relation and consent in "The Sweet Harmony of Christ,"
a sermon preached in 1735 near the peak of the Connecticut Valley Revival, to argue that a "sweet harmony" characterizes the relation between
Christ and the "soul of a true Christian." There is a sweet harmony of
"mutual respect" based on mutual choice, love, and acceptance. There is
a "harmony of likeness or conformity" and thus a commitment to "love
and charity" because we humans look like Christ and like one another.

And there is a "harmony of suitableness," or fitness, based on the relationship between Christ as sovereign Lord and King and believers as obedient subjects. A true Christian should long for this "sweet consent and harmony," this "intimate union," with Christ. The end of the "doctrines and precepts of Christianity," says Edwards, is precisely to bring about harmony between "the soul and Jesus Christ." How "beautiful and lovely," how "inconceivably happy," a Christian will be if he unites and dwells with Christ and "harmony prevails in his soul." This is the only true Christianity. For here, in harmony with Christ, "is to be had joy, that is unspeakable and full of glory."[114]

"Sweet" is Edwards's great modifier, one of the most common words in the Edwardsian lexicon, one he employed in sermons, treatises, and notebooks from early in his career to late, the word he resorted to for imbuing statements about God, grace, and the community of Christians with emotional force. We eat honey, Edwards preaches in 1723, because it is good, "for the sake of its sweetness," for the pleasantness of it, because it is "sweet to your taste."[115] We know honey is sweet not through argumentation or reasoning but through "immediate sensation," by experiencing through taste rather than cogitation in the same way we sense the harmony of a melody emerging from the vibrations of ordered clusters of sound.[116]

And so with spiritual knowledge. While reason may instruct us that the things of nature constitute images of things divine, only saints receiving grace by means of the Holy Spirit gain true vision.[117] Grace, he says, is "sweet to your taste," "as sweet as honey to you." The "sweetness of grace" in the moment we obtain Christ is little different from the pleasantness of Christ, the essence of religion. The beauty of Christ the Mediator is "most sweet," and his love "a sweet fragrancy." The love of God, the Father and friend, "sweetens the comforts" of the godly.[118]

Edwards's metaphors do not always involve literal taste. Believers are "sweetly drawn" by God's love; a mind's succession of thoughts "sweetly corresponds" to God's Word; God's excellence is God's "sweet consent" to himself; holiness is a "sweet, humble . . . and ravishingly" lovely nature that makes the soul a "little, sweet and delightful image" of Jehovah. The Father, Son, and Holy Spirit enjoy among themselves an "infinitely sweet

energy which we call delight"; the Song of Solomon "sweetly" sings the
marriage of Christ and the church of believers; a dear friend's society is
like a "sweet, inexpressibly joyful smile." Fragrant flowers denote "the
sweetnesses of the Son of God!"[119]

These tropes of sweetness convey more than strong sensations from
an individual's taste buds. Sweetness here serves rather to enhance divine attributes such as love, consent, holiness, and energy by making
them seem gentler, more ineffable, more affectionate, more adorable, and
more approachable. The language helps to render God's attributes more
humble than assertive, more attractive and compelling than insistent and
domineering—counterpoints, in fact, to such familiar attributes as overwhelming power and a fierce disposition to judge and punish.

Together they reflect what Edwards recollected in the late 1730s of his
own conversion experiences as a very young man when he began to employ the vocabulary of sweetness. "I used to be a person uncommonly
terrified with thunder," but now it "rejoiced me . . . leading me to sweet
contemplations of my great and glorious God." Walking in the fields he
had a "special Season of uncommon Sweetness." There came, looking
at the sky and clouds, "a sweet Sense of the glorious Majesty and Grace
of GOD . . . sweet and gentle, and holy . . . an awful Sweetness" and a
"high and great, and holy Gentleness."[120] The doctrines of the gospel were
"a sweetness" like "green pastures" to the soul, the "sweetest joys and delights I have experienced." He felt, he recounts, an "inward sweet sense,"
a "sweet conjunction" as though "sweetly conversing" with Christ.[121]

Wayne Lesser provides a useful textual analysis. Edwards writes of himself when a youth as follows: "The heaven I desired was a heaven of holiness" where the saints "could express their love to Christ. I used often to
think, how in Heaven, this sweet principle should freely and fully vent
and express itself." What Edwards longs for, argues Lesser, is a relation
to God beyond his sense of himself (his "I") but that is also beyond the
capacity of language to convey. "Sweet principle," argues Lesser, is a rhetorical solution that "transvalues" the word sweet from the tasting human
self to the divine love that is perfection beyond the words or appetites of
man. It unites opposites—God the divinity and the man Edwards—in
perfect harmony, with their differences at once maintained and recon-
ciled. Where "sweet" had initially reduced holiness to human terms, it

now suggests holiness beyond the human essence. It denotes the young Edwards's longing for sweet "humility" and sweet "calm," where "'sweet communications' with oneself *in* God expresses one's love for Him."[122]

Edwards's fondness for sweetness imagery was not limited to the years of his youth. It appears regularly over the next two decades, as in a sermon on youth and the pleasures of piety, a leitmotif throughout his years in Northampton. Edwards acknowledges that the "life of love" so desired by young people, who especially are "wont to seek pleasure," is the "sweetest life in the world." But like eating honey and honeycomb for the pleasure of it, the practice of virtue and piety is "sweet enough to be its own reward." A life of love is sweet, but love to God is sweeter still, a "purer flame" affording pleasure from a "purer stream." Young people who walk with religion obtain "the sweetest gratification of appetite," not carnal, sensual appetite but excellent, spiritual, divine appetite full of Christ's beauty and the tastes of "angel's food" and "Heaven's dainties," whose gratification is "exquisite, sweet, and delighting," exceeding "the pleasures of the vain, sensual youth, as much as gold and pearls do dirt and dung." Youth is a time when nature blooms and young people naturally care about outward ornaments and their own beauty. Far from hindering such pleasures, embracing religion and virtue promotes them by offering the beauty and ornaments of angels and the "sweetest delights of love and friendship."[123]

People, including youth, should of course have the "sweetest taste" and quickest delight for things the most delightful and less for the less delightful, but Edwards acknowledges that some cannot help themselves, and anyway as fallen humans most are able to taste hardly any sweetness at all.[124] But even for the wicked sunk in luxury, drunkenness, and fornication, there is always repentance, itself a "sweet" sorrow.[125] "Roses grow upon briers" just as "temporal sweets" are always mixed with bitter.[126] The unregenerate will necessarily falter and fail to experience genuine pleasure, and even true Christians must take care lest they glut on sweetness and "vomit it up." But in moderation the "sweet relish" will remain a lifetime.[127]

Sweetness remained important even in periods of revival. In the mid-1730s Edwards asserts the supreme joy of Christ's "sweet harmonies" and the fountain of "sweetest joys" that spills forth when God is present, and at the high tide of the Great Awakening he writes of the emanation of Christ's brightness, the "diffusion of his sweetness," and how his glory and "sweet vivifying influence" are like the coming of spring to the face of the earth. God is the "sweet refreshing light" of God's people and will dress his son in wedding robes. Christ will reveal his "holy, sweet, ravishing beauty" and cover his beloved, the church of saints, with his love. His death for mankind was given as a "sweet smelling savor" to God.[128] As the Awakening recedes in the 1740s, he preaches that an accepting church will rejoice in Christ's divine beauty and "sweetly" solace herself with love to God and one another.[129]

The notion of collectively enjoying sweetness is a refrain in these years. Religion "sweetens temporal . . . pleasures" and enjoyment of "sensitive delights" such as meat, drink, conversation, and recreation. The love, peace, and fellowship of neighbors and feelings of charity to the world serve in the same way. They sweeten the food, drink, and conversation of Christians, a matter of importance because if religion is sweet taken alone it is even more joyful taken in society, where "communion and mutual communications of pleasure do increase it."[130] Scripture underscores this point. When God succored the children of Israel in the wilderness after their escape from Egypt, he told them to draw honey out of bare flinty rock, "sweetness out of the strong," and thereby save themselves till their arrival in Canaan, a land flowing with milk and honey. God's law in the Old Testament in turn had a "sweet smell" acceptable to the senses of the Israelites and thus represented a shadow of the sweet "savor" acceptable to God.[131]

God's presence in the midst of any people adds "sweetness and relish" to what they have, as the presence of God's love among the primitive Christians enabled them to eat their meat together with gladness and singleness of heart.[132] Christ, Edwards says, is also a rock, a foundation to build on and a bulwark of defense from which Christians may draw blessings "exceeding sweet," comparable to "honey and oil, and the best and sweetest" of any earthly Canaan.[133]

The sweetness trope achieved a near apotheosis in the late Northampton years in a memorial volume, which Edwards edited and shepherded to publication, by David Brainerd, a young Edwards acolyte who was a missionary in Connecticut and the mid-Atlantic colonies. The full title of the book is worth attention for its outline, in the splendid eighteenth-century manner, of the essential elements of Brainerd's life and mission: *An Account of the LIFE of the late Reverend Mr. David Brainerd, Minister of the Gospel, Missionary to the Indians, from the honourable Society in Scotland, for the Propagation of Christian Knowledge, and Pastor of a Church of Christian Indians in New-Jersey. Who died at Northampton in New-England, Oct 9th 1747, in the 30th Year of his Age: Chiefly taken from his own Diary, and other private Writings, written for his own Use and now published. By Jonathan Edwards, A. M. 1749.*

Brainerd was a model Christian for Edwards. A New Light of the Great Awakening—so much so that Yale refused to grant him a degree, and a settled ministry was largely beyond reach—Brainerd knew salvation not in an instant, as with the ostentatious revivalists on whom Edwards had soured, but through his steadily growing recognition of God's glory coupled with his own unending sense of humiliation and unworthiness. Salvation when it did arrive was not momentary but enduring, a crucial consideration for Edwards given the backsliding aftermath of the revivals. He therefore applauded Brainerd's unflagging devotion to the task of preaching God's word despite a weak constitution, much physical suffering from frontier conditions, and recurring sorrow from both loneliness and doubt as to the state of his soul. Even though Brainerd often disliked his missionary labors intensely, he persevered, not for himself but for the glory of God.[134]

Moreover, Brainerd's diary is saturated with the language of sweetness. At Yale he writes of a "divine closeness, power and sweetness" and enjoys a "sweetness in religion," an "unspeakable sweetness and delightness in God," a "sweet sense and relish of divine things." For a whole winter his soul seems to "melt into softness," then experiences "divine sweetness," "sensible sweetness," and "Heavenly sweetness" as well as sweet refreshment, Heaven, consolation, and "nothingness." Brainerd's twenty-fourth birthday is "a sweet, a happy day" to him, with his soul "enlarged in sweet intercession for my fellowmen everywhere." And so on, to the end of his life.[135]

Brainerd is not Edwards, and his imagery cannot be literally taken for Edwards's. The diary is at one remove from Edwards's writings. Yet Edwards was close to Brainerd and followed and endorsed his labors.

Edwards's daughter Jerusha nursed Brainerd in his final illness. Brainerd died in the Edwards home. And Edwards saw to the diary's publication, making it a high priority at a very stressful time near the end of his Northampton ministry. It was clearly a meaningful work for him, and its expressions seem in a certain sense to belong to Edwards, who writes in the *Life* of Brainerd's "inward sweetness and breathing after God," his "seasons of divine sweetness and comfort," his "composure, calmness, resignation, ardent desire and sweet fervency of spirit," his "spiritual sweetness in conversation," his "holy temper and Heavenly disposition," his "sweet and grateful frame of mind," and in the end his "ineffable sweetness and comfort."[136]

The Life of David Brainerd offers us the portrait of a kind, compassionate, sweet, gentle Christian man, a symbol of true faith doing his self-sacrificial duty wholly for the adoration of God. The *Life* became in the next century the most widely owned of all the works of Jonathan Edwards.

This brief journey through the tropes of sweetness, harmony, beauty, and light does not annul the received Edwardsian personae. He was still an intellectual, a Calvinist, a revivalist, and a scold—but only in part and of a kind. His imagery and concepts and the uses he made of them reveal him to have been incomparably more—more tender, more sensitive, more poetic and perceptive and receptive not only to Scripture and the call of Heaven but to the natural and social worlds around him, a point that will become clearer in the chapters to come.

4

CHARITY

When I think of the poverty and misery in the midst of us, and all the consequences thereof, I hardly dare feel grateful for the princely fortunes some men have gathered together. Certainly it is not a Christian society, where such extremes exist.

— THEODORE PARKER

To UNDERSTAND the centrality of charity in Edwards's thought and ministry requires a few words more about Puritanism and "works," of which charity was one of the most important. Puritans adhered to a doctrine of free unearned grace: God, omnipotent and omniscient, would bestow salvation on depraved sinners regardless of merit. Good works, whether for church or community or individuals, would play no role in regeneration. To think otherwise—to assume that human endeavor could affect one's prospects for sainthood—would elevate individuals and denigrate the power of God. The result would be either the Arminian doctrine of individual human empowerment and worth that Jonathan Edwards and other New England ministers rejected or, worse, the Catholic doctrine of grace through works that had produced, Puritans thought, the vast corruptions of the Roman Catholic Church.

But that was not the end of the matter because the notion of God's omnipotence implied predestination, which seemed on its face to leave no room for ministers to urge people to a more powerful sense of sin, a greater faith, more piety, and better behavior, all of them theoretically irrelevant to regeneration. "If I am elected," Jonathan Edwards imagines a parishioner saying—imagines it in all likelihood because he had heard, or knew other ministers had heard, precisely such a comment—"I shall be saved, and if not, I shall be damned, let me do what I will." Edwards says in response, "Don't imagine yourself excused simply because of God's

51

absolute decrees, from the diligent use of the means of your salvation." In other words, work at it anyway.[1]

Sensing the inadequacy of "work at it anyway" as a rejoinder, ministers, including Edwards, struggled to find a better solution to the tension between God's omnipotence and human effort. They came up with several. One was the concept of God's "covenant" with his chosen people, the Israelites—the bestowing of blessings on the community in return for adherence to the commandments and universal moral law. New England Puritans of the seventeenth century considered themselves a covenant people, too, and this opened a fertile field for pulpit imprecation and exhortation that Edwards and others exploited by ascribing, for example, bad weather, epidemics, the fall of Cromwell's government, fires and building collapses, and setbacks at the hands of the French to God's punishment of covenant-breaking sinners. Edwards, says Harry Stout, adhered "exactly" to this notion of New England as "peculiar" and a "city upon a hill" because covenanted of God.[2]

In addition, there was the presumption that "natural" unjustified men have a conscience and therefore the capacity to know and be expected to try to follow the "moral law" that God had embedded in all humans at the creation and that was codified as "the Law" of the Old Testament commandments. Ministers urged adherence to this law by appealing to basic conscience to the extent they thought efficacious. Edwards spent much time considering this concept of obedience to moral law, differentiating, for example, Jewish "ceremonial" law from both the law of Christian "righteousness" and the "sense of beauty in moral things," and also articulating a rationale for demanding good behavior from the irreligious and unchurched.[3]

The most common solution, at least in the early eighteenth century, was the practice of Edwards, Solomon Stoddard, and their peers of preaching the importance of "preparation," of adhering to Christian values and behavior, the natural law of conscience, and achieving a conviction of personal sin as a way to ready oneself—"prepare"—for the influx of grace. Terror sermons were of course one way to induce preparation; so were sermons prescribing pious behavior. This approach may not have been strictly logical from a Calvinist standpoint, but it did make practical sense because it tended to shift responsibility for attitudes and behavior away from the community as a whole to the individual person whose soul was ultimately at issue. Most preachers of Edwards's day employed prepa-rationism along with conscience and the covenant to push their congre-gations to improve their communities and their lives, although usually favoring by this time in New England history the need to prepare. As Edwards put it early in his career, "The exercise of grace is given entirely by the Spirit of God . . . [but] his ordinary method, notwithstanding, is to give grace to those that are much concerned about it and . . . continue to do things in order to it."[4]

All this meant that even for Puritans who preached salvation as a matter finally between the individual and God, a conviction of sin and works in the sense of visible evidences of true faith was never irrelevant. Edwards in particular came to argue, especially in the difficult days following the Connecticut Valley Revival and the Great Awakening, that a worshiper's personal testimony about rebirth, even if heartfelt and sincere, is ultimate-ly just words. Works are the true test, the surest overt sign of justification. Works might not actually *bring* justification, but works would *inevitably accompany* justification. Edwards says, assessing the Great Awakening, that there is "a sort of external religious practice, wherein there is no inward experience," which is good for nothing; and there is "experience, that is without practice," which is "worse than nothing."[5]

All the precepts that Christ followed "may [be] reduced to one law," the "great and everlasting law of God" known as the "covenant of works."[6] "To be a Christian really," Edwards asserts, "is to have . . . [both] the profession of faith, and outward holiness in the visible life and conversa-tion."[7] The Christian zeal so evident in the revivals should drive men to be zealous of good works, to be "ardent" to do something "whereby God may be pleased and honored."[8] In the formulation of William Breiten-bach, Edwards believed that "virtue to be true must be gracious" and that "grace to be true must be virtuous." The one attests to the other.[9]

Edwards thought that two types of works should be visible in the lives of the sanctified. There should first be acts of respect for God—external expressions of inward fear, reverence, trust, and obedience. These should include "outward prayer, singing psalms, going to the public assemblies of God's people, attending the sacraments, keeping days of fasting or thanksgiving, reading and hearing the word of God, attending private re-ligious meetings, speaking respectfully of God, talking much of God and Christ, and seeming affectionate and reverential in the manner of our talk of things of religion or in our manner of behavior" in worship.[10] Under this same heading of steadfast visible piety would also come, as a kind of subordinate adjunct, the various "thou shalt nots" of illicit, disrespectful, licentious, "wicked" behavior that peppered the sermons: bawdy singing, mockery of religion, tavern-keeping and heavy drinking, "frolics," night visiting, rowdiness during meeting and other "polluting wickedness" that constituted not only a perpetual temptation for young people but a distraction from devotion to God for everyone.[11]

The second type of the works of the saints is charity, the inevitable corollary and consequence of genuine love to God that flows from and demonstrates the gift of grace, the true hallmark of the sanctified life. No virtue save love for Christ is greater than charity, no sin save rejection of Christ worse than lack of charity. "They that do good to others shall be rewarded whether to their souls or bodies." Souls would always and obviously be a priority, as for all New England ministers. But "they that do good to others' outward man shall not lose their reward."[12] Charity is the certain sign of the "Christian temper," the "one grace" related to all graces, the hard "rule" of mercy and benevolence, the "sum of all saving virtue."[13] The more light any doctrine or institution sheds on the spiritual world, says Edwards, "the more will it urge to love and charity."[14] Charity is nothing less than "true grace" with its "seat in the heart."[15]

Genuine religious zeal is therefore not so much revival ecstasy as "fervent hearty Christian charity," a zeal "not against men but against sin— their sins earnestly opposed but their persons fervently loved."[16] Charity, a gift of the "ordinary saving influence" of the Spirit, is "far preferable" to the "extraordinary" gifts of prophecy and tongues that occurred at the time of the apostles, and *only* at that time, according to Edwards, clearly reacting to revivalist excesses.[17] The essential evidence of true grace is "good works of charity," the "love of brethren." The primary fruit of the Spirit is "love and charity, a "merciful spirit and practice," a "Christian temper and behavior towards ourselves and our fellow creatures."[18]

By charity, Edwards sometimes means generosity of spirit—assuming the best of persons and taking them to be potential brethren in faith or common humanity, a stance that would be evidence, as in the quotation above, of a "Christian temper." He also uses it, following the strict

translation of the Greek *agape,* to mean love in its most encompassing
sense of disposition or affection to men and to God, a usage that constitutes, as we shall discuss, the centerpiece and quintessence of his vision
of holiness. Most of the time, especially in his sermons, charity means
simply what the word would have meant in a practical sense in the lives
of his congregation: the giving of one's wealth, whether goods or money,
to relieve human needs, especially the needs of the poor.[19] Do good "in
ways of charity to the poor. He that gives to the poor lends to the Lord."[20]
Christ "accepts" giving to the poor as "being done to himself."[21] Bestow
your earthly goods "on the poor, who are God's receivers." If bestowed on
"the least" of Christ's brethren, " 'tis bestowed on Christ."[22]

The duties of charity, humility, meekness, and patience are "gospel duties," the "sum of what God requires of us."[23] "That brotherly charity that
is due to visible saints" is "the bond by which the several members of the
church of Christ are united," but the net reaches well beyond the saints:
"Of all the external things that we can do to have the spirit of God continued amongst [us], I believe the most likely thing to be successful to
that end, of any one thing whatsoever, is abounding in deeds of love and
charity."[24] Holiness, that most blessed state, comprehends all the true virtue of a good man, including "his love to God, his gracious love to men,
his justice, his charity and bowels of mercies." This means, he specifies,
"liberality to the poor" and "bounty to the poor."[25]

Care for the poor rather than the scramble for wealth and honor is
a noticeable element of the Edwardsian message as early as 1723 when
he warns his little New York congregation that if "you are uncharitable"
and "neglect the welfare of your fellow-creatures" or refuse to distribute
"necessities" to others and fail to help "fellow-Christians," that is selfish
and un-Christian. We are all "God's own," we should remember, and
bear his "image and likeness," so that giving to the poor instead of to
"your outward ease and prosperity" is the same as giving to God himself,
the true owner, after all, of everything you possess.[26] Underscoring the
point, he describes a master who "cruelly" deals with his servant, forcing
him to labor "hard" and "without ceasing" for "nothing," not even food
or clothing, because the master himself is in thrall to sin, which makes
him as "barbarous" as an owner of slaves who works them to death in the
mines or in chains.[27]

These arguments—the importance of human welfare, the plight of the poor, the selfishness of not helping, the likeness of the poor to God, God's injunction to charity, God's ownership of all things—would become standard for Edwards, who became more insistent, assertive, and directive about them as he settled into his Northampton ministry. Works performed in a "spirit of charity towards men" as "labors of love" signal the reality of grace, and we should "sell all" to perform them.[28] God requires "a liberal and bountiful disposition," a "care and concern for the good of others," rather than a "fearful" and "private-spirited" cowardice. Even more, a Christian temper means not only to be of "a liberal and bountiful disposition" and to give for the "greater good," but to do so out of *real* love and "inward charity" rather than to "dissemble" about it as (he says pointedly) some men do.[29]

The same kind of message inflects sermons on other topics. Thus, mercy and charity are "proper and acceptable to Christ" on the Sabbath. Following Christ demands meekness and obedience, but it also demands charity. A Christian should exercise a spirit of "free, universal, and disinterested love and beneficence and Christian charity," and avoid envy and jealousy as not only evil in themselves but contradictory to a charitable "spirit."[30] The first paragraph of Edwards's account of the Awakening of the early 1740s in Northampton mentions the "evident alteration with respect to a charitable spirit to the poor."[31]

"The Duty of Charity to the Poor," a 1733 sermon preached over four meetings, was an extended elaboration of the topic. Edwards begins by quoting Deuteronomy and Leviticus on the duty to help the poor, including those outside one's community, even if they are one's enemies, and on helping freely without expecting a benefit. Doing otherwise, refusing to succor "thy poor brother," would be "base" and engender well-deserved guilt. The charity must be plentiful and at the same time not begrudging, a "liberal gift" appropriate to need, because to give sparingly is "no manifestation of charity" at all. God has commanded this duty in a "peremptory, urgent" voice: "I know of scarce any particular duty that is so much insisted upon, so pressed and urged upon us, both in the Old Testament and New."[32]

"Your money" and "your goods" are not actually yours in any case, but God's. Giving to the poor, the very emblems of Christ on earth, is therefore merely to return it to its rightful owner. If Christ was here among us, suffering and in "calamitous and needy circumstances" like so many, we would surely supply him and them and should do so now. Consider, too, that you or your children might someday experience this kind of poverty in so "shifting, changing, uncertain" a world, and want bread that you once refused to others.

Much of this is reiteration of points made a decade earlier, but Edwards here adds an emphasis on social unity and the family of man, a concept that grows over the years to acquire immense significance for him. We are brothers made in God's image, allied by nature, of "one blood," with like faculties, subject to the same feelings and "aversion to misery." We are made to "subsist by society and union." Otherwise we perish. Help to others preserves human society and humanity itself. A selfish "private" spirit of resistance to charity is suitable only for "wolves and beasts of prey." People with this attitude deserve to be "cut off from the benefit of human society." Therefore search yourselves to see whether you have coveted your wealth or given grudgingly or "shut up the bowels of your compassion." If so, he warns, the God who commands you to charity may curse you.[33]

In the longest of the four parts of the sermon, Edwards itemizes and responds to possible objections from townspeople to charity to the poor. It is a remarkable list, providing a glimpse of Northampton social attitudes and also of Edwards's evolving social ethic, which, as Mark Valeri rightly says, verged on privileging social action over evangelical theology.[34] Some of the objections and responses are fairly conventional for the time but still worth noting. Taken as a whole, they address to an astounding degree concerns about helping the poor that persist in virtually identical terms into the twenty-first century.

If those of us who are as yet unjustified "natural" men are charitable in spite of our spiritual state, goes the first of these objections, won't we preen and strut and feel superior because we gave, thereby committing the terrible sin of pride that you have warned us against? Charity, answers Edwards, is a part of the common moral law, on a par with the commandments against murder and theft and a part of the common natural conscience that everyone possesses. God expects charity from even the unsaved, just as he expects everyone to obey the Ten Commandments.

Will giving then help me personally in some way, as some ministers sometimes say? Possibly, but only in God's time, not yours, and only if the gift is ungrudging.

Should we give even to people who are perhaps needy but are not in severe "extremity"? Yes. They are our neighbors, travelers with us in the direction of grace, whom we should love as ourselves even if they do not have "broken bones."[35]

How about "ill-tempered" and "ungrateful" people who have treated us badly? Do we have to give to them, too? Yes. Consider that Christ loved us even though we are ourselves hateful sinners. We must aspire to do the same.

What if we do not have enough money or property for ourselves? If you are rich, you must provide from your bounty without worrying about the future. God will provide, if not here then in Heaven. If you are poor, a cup of water out of poverty is the same to God as riches out of wealth. "Enough" is in any case relative and largely in the eye of the beholder.[36]

But how do we know that someone is truly needy? Learn what you can, says Edwards, but if you are in doubt, help anyway: " 'Tis better to give to several that are not objects of charity, than to send away empty one that is."[37]

Shouldn't the poor, though, be expected to ask us directly for help if they need it? No, says Edwards. That would force them to become beggars, something that you would dislike if you were poor, and it would not be "agreeable to the liberal man," who should search out the needy on his own. "To [be] put upon begging in order to [receive] relief is . . . a real difficulty; and we should, any of us, look upon it so. It is more charitable, more brotherly, more becoming Christians and the disciples of Jesus, to do it without. I think it is self-evident, and needs no proof." Leave the needy with their dignity.

Should we help even if a poor person is poor through his own fault? If by "fault" is meant incompetence in managing his affairs, responds Edwards, "that [incompetence] is his calamity" as much as if he had no feet or eyesight. Those who have feet and eyes and wisdom should help those who do not. If a man was imprudent, even idle or prodigal, and mends his ways, the rules of the gospel still require charity. Even if he does not in the end mend his ways, we must continue to assist at least his family.[38]

Why, the objections continue, should we help when others are not do-ing their share and may even have somehow themselves caused the man's poverty, through for example harsh or unfair dealings? That makes no dif-ference. You must still assist whoever is in need, as the Samaritan did the poor Jew when no one else would. If others are doing too little, the need will be all the greater, and your response should be greater as well.

But why should we as private persons succor the poor when the law obliges the town to provide charity? This objection, rejoins Edwards, rests on the false premise that towns help everyone who is in need. In fact, that usually means only those reduced to absolute "extremity" with no land or capacity whatsoever. There are many perhaps less desperate than this but still in "pinching" want and requiring our charity. The law is not intended to "cut off all occasion for Christian charity." The law is needed because "voluntary charity in this corrupt world" is uncertain. "Let the design of the law be what it will . . . 'tis too obvious to be denied that there are in fact those that are in want. . . . A man must hide his eyes to think other-wise."[39] Public assistance is essential, but Christian charity will be always essential as well, appropriate and enjoined by God.

"The Duty of Charity to the Poor" elaborates Edwards's sense of who should receive charity. Not all the needy are in "extremity" or desperate. Some are in temporary want, some less than abject, the victims of busi-ness conditions, natural disaster, or bad judgment. He notes elsewhere that a rich man with sudden "great losses" may actually need more help, like Job, than men who are chronically poor and thus perhaps more ac-customed to penury. He also urges "liberality to ministers of the gospel" who are not poor yet need "comfortable and honorable support" to do their work in the same way that "priests of old lived upon sacrifices that were offered to God." Ministerial work is demanding enough in fact to bear comparison to "the ox that labors in a man's husbandry." The one brings forth spiritual food, the other corn. Both require sustenance.[40] You owe "gifts" of charity to any fellow Christian as an act of love. But show "liberality" to ministers of the gospel, for Christ looks upon charity to ministers, like charity to the poor, "as offered to himself."[41]

Yet the poor are always Edwards's main focus. "God hath chosen the poor of this world," he says in 1731 as he had in 1723, and "none but the poor of this world," to be the "joint-heirs with Jesus Christ."[42] Even unregenerate natural men following the "common duties and offices of humanity" ought to relieve them when they are "sick" or under "distress" and need the benefits of human society and "the support of life."[43] It is shameful for a Christian to be "backward and strait-handed" to his "poor brethren," to whom he must rather "abound" in deeds of charity. Christians must show "liberality" and "bounty" to "the poor," however "mean and abject" they appear. And as always, he that gives "bountifully" to the poor, the "least of his brethren," lends to the Lord and will receive back, if not in this life then in eternity: "What rewards are promised" to those who do good "to the bodies of men, that give to the poor" and thus "lend to the Lord."[44]

Edwards's preoccupation with the poor emerges as well from his unvarying, at times almost obsessive, description of Christ incarnate as one of the poor. Christ was born in a "low condition" in a "manger," the livestock feeder of a stable, to a "poor virgin" of "strait and difficult" circumstance who was without "conveniences" and married to a "poor man, a carpenter." Christ too followed the "mechanical trade" of carpentry, earning his bread through "hard labor" and remaining "poor" so that his "poverty" might enrich us. He lived an "obscure life among laboring men," no more noticed than other "common laborers" and "mean ordinary men" until John baptized him, after which he still endured "great poverty" and slept in the open. In such circumstances he was "doubtless often pinched with hunger and cold," despised as a "poor, insignificant" person of "little account," with "low parentage and a "mean" city of birth. He was in so "low and needy" a state that he depended on the "charity of his followers" to sustain life. Pilate and Herod both considered him "worthless." He died on the cross like a "slave and malefactor," like the "meanest and worst of vagabonds and miscreants," mocked and tortured as the "vilest of creatures" until he expired between two notorious thieves in a place for the punishment of criminals.[45] The beauty of Christ, a "poor, obscure, despised, afflicted man," was precisely in his "meekness" and "lowliness" and "condescension to the mean and vile, and compassion to the miserable."[46]

In a typological gloss on Isaiah of the kind Edwards relished, he says that Christ did not appear as a great man, as a "tall cedar," but as a "meaner" sort, "one of the lesser and lower sort of plants," a "small tender twig" liable to suffer and exposed to malice, a "branch" that might easily bruise or break rather than a "stiff strong tree." He possessed none of the "outward glory" of a tree that grows "high, and large, and flourishing in its pride" and rises in a "fat soil" with a multitude of flowing waters at its roots. He was drawn rather from "dry ground," a root that grows low, spreads little, and is devoid of "gay appearance." Lacking "form, or comeliness, or beauty," he was a bush or weak plant without the pomp and glory of tall trees and earthly princes.[47]

This portrayal of Jesus as poor, despised, and afflicted is particularly prominent in a sermon series from the late 1730s, the "dull" time between the Connecticut Valley Revival and the Great Awakening after the congregation's decision to assign pews at the new meeting house largely on the basis of wealth.[48] Present everywhere in Edwards's work, the special intensity of the depiction of Christ as impoverished in these sermons may serve as a measure of the intensity of his annoyance with prosperous Northampton.[49]

Edwards portrays Mary, the mother of Christ, as of low birth and in need.[50] He portrays the disciples and apostles in similar terms—a company of "poor fishermen," persons of "low education," "unschooled, workers, fishermen," "illiterate, simple, undesigning, ignorant" men with no knowledge of the scheme of salvation and gospel, surviving on the meager resources of the primitive Christian churches, which were themselves so poor in the beginning that some, particularly in Asia, survived on the charity of others.[51] The earliest Lord's Suppers, he argues, were partly charitable feasts intended "for the poorest and meanest." The church at Corinth earned Paul's condemnation for turning away the hungry.[52] The immediate followers of the apostles as teachers of the word of Christ also lived on the "substance of others," eventually numbering so many that they had of necessity possessed "all things common."[53] The office of deacon originated to care for the "outward supply of the members of Christ's church, and the exercise of that great Christian virtue of charity."[54]

Edwards notes that most of the beneficiaries of Christ's miracles were either sick with leprosy or other bodily "corruptions" or else mute, blind, or lame. The miracles were therefore "works of mercy" for people who were among the poorest of the poor, as the sick and broken invariably are in all societies, and Edwards singles them out as needing help in Northampton and New England like anywhere else. They thus become a part of the pool of area poor people who are landless, "indigent," even beggars—"too obvious," he asserts against possible indifference, to miss. He includes as well "the widow, the fatherless, the stranger," all biblical types confronting poverty who would be familiar in any New England town, including Northampton, and in any part of the British Empire, and he adds for good measure the "meek" and "broken-hearted" and the "captive" and "imprisoned," drawing again from Scripture but with reference as well to the surrounding environment.[55]

One of the communities of earlier Christian times whose story Edwards relates favorably was the Waldenses, a separatist group (Edwards offers the opinion that they "appear Protestant") living deep in the Piedmont region that resisted control from Rome despite repeated assaults, and surviving, though in poverty, by "the strictness of their lives, for charity and other Christian virtues." The "Romanists" eventually drove them into other parts of Europe, only to hound and persecute them again during the Counter-Reformation. The Reformation itself, Edwards reminds us, attracted the "illiterate" and "weak," including women and children.[56]

The poor are not only recipients of alms but also, Edwards argues in a sermon from the 1740s, models of Christian humility—humble like Christ himself, unassuming like Christ, respectful of superiors and obedient to authority like Christ and as befits their situation. They are patient with "hard fare" and subdued to "hard things," but neither "stiff and self-willed" nor prone to "resentment." A poor man is "modest in his speech and behavior" like a true Christian, and "humble . . . amongst men." Accustomed to be a subject, Edwards continues, a poor man "don't take it heinously" if he is ignored, as he usually is. He is humble, and through humility he is "disposed . . . to honor" not just saints but "all men."[57] These remarks without a doubt idealize the poor, though probably not as much as it might seem since they reflect the genuinely deferential habits still lingering in colonial North America that Edwards thought best for Christian, and every other, society.

Edwards was an acute observer of his community—"I have had [more] opportunity of very extensive observation than any other person in the town"—and knew that there were many poor people that the community was obligated to sustain by Massachusetts Bay law.[58] One dimension of Christian faith and adherence to the moral law was support on behalf of taxation for public assistance, a requirement that Edwards not only never questioned but labored to supplement, believing as he did that the better-off were obliged not only by colonial and municipal law but by God's commandment to relieve the needs of the poor. Voluntary charity was a supplement but a crucial and indispensable one.

In 1742, after years of effort, he persuaded the town to establish a community welfare fund under the church deacons. Just a year later, he called on rich families to give not less than 25 percent of their total wealth to charity and to provide, moreover, scholarships and schools for the poor, which he had heard that some rich German Protestants were doing.

By what measure, after all, should we judge Christian behavior, he preaches in explanation? By how many poor there are in a place. And how many would that be? "None."[59] In the language of our own era, Edwards was an advocate for a safety net and a system of both taxation and tithing that would redistribute a significant measure of wealth from the rich to the poor, ultimate proof, in Edwards's eyes, of the validity of protestations of faith.

Edwards understood that the poor commonly think of themselves the same way others think of them—as essentially marginal people. "You may be [held] in but little esteem, may be despised and slighted and accounted of no great consequence in the world, and have not that respect shewn to you that many of your neighbours have." You may be "weak in understanding" and "comparatively ignorant," and are "not much accounted of, you see that your judgment of things is not so much taken notice of, your voice is not so much heard as others on public affairs." But Christ, too, was "low in the world" like you and has sent his ministers to "gather you up." You that are poor and have a "smaller part of the good things of this life" than most of your neighbors, and are "hard put" to provide necessities for yourself and your family, and are often "reduced to straits and difficulties"—you should hark to Christ's call. "If you are mea[n]ly clad and forced to wear that which is coarse and homely. . . . If you live upon mean fare and sometimes are pinched with hunger," even if you are "servants and poor negroes," come to Christ "and you shall not have mean fare. . . . And when you have done with the world, when those things fail, you shall be received into everlasting habitations, where you shall hunger no more."[60]

Edwards sometimes suggests that the poor have a role to play and deserve to be included in the life of the town. He argues that "a poor man in a cottage that walks with God" might do little in public affairs yet still play a part, through fervent prayer, to keep the covenant with God, "more, it may be, than some of the great men with their power and policy." Men of wealth, learning, and honor "ben't of so great value" in God's eyes as poor persons who are "not much regarded" and have little chance to glorify Christ. But like the biblical widow who cast her two mites into the treasury, the "poorest, meanest" person in the congregation can do something—and Christ will notice.[61] Though "mean and obscure . . . little known and taken notice of," a poor man may be a "public blessing" who brings down "showers of blessing on all around him." The poor, unlike "wicked private persons" who pull down God's judgment on the land, are, to echo Christ, "the salt of the land, preserving it [from] spoiling and coming to ruin." Kings and the rich may give to the poor and build stately churches, but if they lack love to God it means less than "the sincere, secret devotion of a poor, obscure Christian."[62]

Amy Schrager Lang argues that this propensity to include, though perhaps faint in some modern eyes, differentiates Edwards from ministerial adversaries such as Charles Chauncy of Boston, who attacked the revivals on the grounds that they threatened "to destroy all property" and swept up not only the illiterate poor but women, girls, even "Negroes," as of course they did.[63] Supporting this point is Edwards's request to the male elite on the presiding church committee at the time of his dismissal that he be allowed to defend from the pulpit his position against open communion. He had written a short book summarizing his position, but argued that "there are others, both male and female, to whom I have stood in so sacred a relation," who "it can never be expected that they should generally read my pamphlet," partly because they refused to read it but also because some were illiterate or lacked funds to buy the book or connections to borrow it.[64] He thought afterwards that if women and young people had been allowed to vote on his dismissal, he might not have lost (though hard evidence for this is scant).[65] The "main thing" Christ came into the world for, "the blessed effect he had respect to in all he said and did" and which "crowns it all," was "the poor's being evangelized." Christ was encouraged to see among his converts "the poorer sort, not many wise, not many mighty," including husbandmen and ploughmen, the standbys of the rustic worlds of Jesus and Edwards.[66]

Not only did revivals and awakenings draw from the ranks of the less well-to-do, but Edwards was candid about trying to appeal to them in his hellfire sermons, noting that God works mainly through fear "in the more unthinking people, such as husbandmen and the common sort of people."[67] Robert Lee Stuart says this shows a clear class bias.[68] But Edwards characterizes Christ and his disciples and apostles in much the same way, and he goes on to argue that someone of a "humble, or meek, or charitable" spirit, though of "mean capacity," will actually follow the Christian dispensation sooner than someone of "strong faculties" without this spirit.[69] There is a certain antique consciousness of class (or rank or orders) in Edwards, as Perry Miller and other scholars have suggested, but the statement above is as much accurate perception as harsh bias. Edwards may have been ultimately a kind of visionary reformer, but in some ways he was a sober realist: every society in the history of the world has had ranks. What matters is what kind.

In his first extended description of the Connecticut Valley Revival, Edwards praises Phoebe Bartlett, his four-year-old convert, for asking her father to help a "poor man" living in the woods who lost a cow and consequently found his family in much reduced straits. This request, says Edwards, shows Phoebe's "bowels of compassion for the poor," which he takes to be evidence of true charity and therefore genuine regeneration. Phoebe has always attracted readers' attention in this account, but it is worth noting that the recipient is one of the community's poor men, living in the woods close enough to the Bartletts to visit, and it is perhaps worth noting, too, that in Northampton as in all marginal agrarian societies the death of a single cow could plunge a family into "pinching want." There are also the Bartletts themselves. Mrs. Bartlett at one point asks Phoebe if she wants to go to God's church to see "fine folks," a comment suggesting that the Bartlett family was far from the social heights, perhaps offering a modest validation of Edwards's comment about appealing to "common people."[70]

One reason for Edwards's propensity to idealize the poor was rhetorical—to allow him to hammer the rich, his favorite target for warnings and condemnation, people who, in contrast to the poor, are prone to "answer roughly," are "haughty" and "impudent," and are infected with pride and "counterfeit humility."[71] Edwards loves to juxtapose the well-to-do and the poor, worldliness and charity, covetousness and generosity. The "exalted" of this world will be "lowest in hell," by far the "lowest," because they are "hypocrites" who make "a show of being God's worshippers" and a "pretense of regard to the poor" under "a cloak of covetousness." And caring for souls is no substitute, says, significantly, this famous revivalist. Making a "great shew" of love and pity, after all, "costs'em nothing," as they well know, while showing "mercy to men's bodies" means "money out of their pockets."[72]

Some swear they would die for God, yet will not "suffer a little in their estates and names and worldly convenience. . . . [They] han't confidence enough in God to dare to trust him with a little of their estates, bestowed to pious and charitable use."[73] Officeholders seek their "private interest more than the interest of the public," aim to "enrich and advance themselves," and make the "public weal" their "private designs."[74] Some "injure others in their estates by unfairness in their dealings," by being "fraudulent and deceitful," by "taking advantage of their necessities." They show a "selfish spirit," are "all for themselves," are "servants of Mammon," have "no regard to the good or benefit of their neighbor." You make excuses, he accuses from the pulpit, about having "bought oxen" to "feed and sell," or land that you must "go and see," refusing Christ's injunction for the sake of "your farms or your cattle." A "pretense of regard to the poor" often cloaks "covetousness."[75]

Satan himself "dissuades men from parting with some of their estates for the benefit of their neighbors in want, or for some public service," and disparages "bountifulness and liberality" as "prodigality" and therefore sin. Some men are "all for themselves" without regard for the "good or benefit of their neighbor. . . . [A]ll their contrivance is to aggrandize themselves." Their spirit is "selfish."[76] Edwards condemns with particular bitterness the nefarious but apparently common practice of giving depreciated currency to charity, thereby "cheating the church of God and defrauding the expectation of the poor," who stand, as everyone knows, as "Christ's receivers." Those who purposely use "bad money" for contributions know it would not be accepted in payment of public taxes and their "neighbours won't accept it." They therefore try to "save themselves by putting it off to God."[77]

"If you are uncharitable," he admonishes in an early sermon, "if you neglect the welfare of your fellow-creatures; if you are not ready, freely and without grudging, to distribute to the needs and necessities of others; if you withhold your hand from doing good to your fellow-Christians upon all occasions for a needless fear of hurting yourself," you are acting "as if you were your own" and demonstrating what God abhors: selfishness, worldliness, and pride. He quotes Christ from Matthew to seal the point: "Inasmuch as ye have done it to one of the least of my brethren, ye have done it unto me."[78] And he draws on Matthew to remind parishioners that the rich "must become as poor as the poorest when death calls 'em away from their riches." They must then leave "all their money, all their honor; their pleasures and friends, their houses and lands, and whatever else they had," a point he continuously reiterates.[79]

Edwards disparages the vanity of wealth and "fashionable" education, ascribes the prevalence of "malice, envy, and revenge" to "covetousness," compares the scramble for worldly riches and power to a scramble for what God scatters before "dogs," warns that the Day of Judgment will bring punishment for "business fraud."[80] He says that the modern art of navigation, "a great potential blessing" to commerce and communication, is currently being "improved . . . in fear, with covetousness and pride . . . by wicked, debauched men." Salvation is meanwhile "made nothing of" in comparison to "worldly gain, or gay clothing, or youthful diversions."[81]

Let the "rich," in view of their weighty influence, be "exhorted" from wickedness.[82] Men are diligent to protect and preserve the "accommodations and entertainments of a convenient, beautiful, well-furnished habitation, and to partake of the provisions and produce of a plentiful estate" for a day or two without worrying about eternity. They know how to "adjust things in their dealings and contracts" in temporal matters with no care for their immortal souls. Farmers carefully plow and sow and harvest for a good crop, merchants are "eagle-eyed" to improve opportunities and "enrich" themselves, men will not sleep for fearing damage to their "worldly estate." Yet they fail meanwhile to attend the prospect of salvation.[83]

Does God have nothing better to bestow upon you than "a little money or land"? "If you have more land than some of your neighbours, a larger stock, and more comfortable and plentiful accommodations" but lack grace, you will be miserable. "When you look upon your buildings, your cattle, your stores," you should "consider that brimstone is scattered upon them all," and when you sit at a full table," there is "God's bow bent."[84] Sin makes men think another "two or three hundred pounds" will make them "great gainers," even though they will "lose themselves forever" in hell as payment.[85] If people are "cold and unconcerned" about religion, "injustice, and fraud, and oppression will grow." If men contend, it is usually about "the world and worldly things." But if they are religious, they are "not so much disposed" to conflict over "their profit and their honor."[86]

Edwards sees countless lessons about wealth in the New Testament, as when Mark recounts how the Jews esteemed "their great men that were rich" and therefore did not believe that the "poorer, meaner sort" of "low" esteem who followed Christ were likely to enter the kingdom. According to Luke, Christ "greatly contradicted" these notions with the parable of the rich descendant of Abraham who found himself shut out while Lazarus, "a poor stranger," was admitted.[87] Matthew recounts how Christ told a rich man to sell his goods and give everything to the poor if he would enter Heaven; but he would not and therefore did not.[88] Timothy relates how hard it is for the rich, with "much to beat them back," to gain Heaven. James says a rich man "made low by poverty" from persecution actually rejoiced at this blessing.[89] Paul criticizes "those that were rich" in Corinth for consuming all that was provided while the "poor were sent away without anything."[90] And Edwards invokes not only the Beatitudes but Christ's famous warning in Mark that a camel will pass through a needle's eye before the wealthy enter the kingdom of God.[91]

Edwards's criticism of wealth, worldliness, and profit-seeking fluctuated a little from decade to decade. To oversimplify from impressionistic evidence, there was a gentle surge in the early 1720s and a stronger one from the late 1720s to the early 1730s, a slight ebbing in the mid-1730s when much of his focus was on the soul, a surge in the late 1730s at the time of the bitter meeting house pew dispute, a flattening during the Awakening of the early 1740s, and a surge for a few years thereafter. The hated pew decision in 1737 may help explain one of these surges. Some, he intones in his most caustic manner, have more "stately houses," are "richer," possess "higher offices" than others, and have "higher seats in the meetinghouse." But death awaits you all: "One rotting, putrefying corpse" resembles the other, and "the worms are as bold with one carcass" as the next. You prize "one seat before another in the house of worship" because it is . . . reckoned first in number" when you should be seeking a mansion with God above. You are "pleased" with your seats because you are "seated high" in a place that looks "honorable" to those around and behind you. Well, you will enjoy this pleasure but a "short time." It is but "a little while before it will [be] all one to you, whether you have sat high or low."[92]

And so on even three years after the pew decision: "Now you sit forward in the meeting house, and have a higher seat than your poor, inferior neighbours, yet hereafter you shall be set in a lower place in hell than those wicked men who now sit behind you." Consider this before you "go away, one to his farm and another to his merchandize."[93] It seems plausible to suggest that Edwards never entirely recovered from this episode, which represented, by its enshrining of wealth, an institutional rejection of his vision of other forms of honor and worth and foretold the long gradual estrangement of pastor and congregation that ended in dismissal.[94]

In 1742, anxious that the Great Awakening might have no more lasting transformative effect than the Connecticut Valley Revival of the mid-1730s, he went to the unprecedented extreme of drafting a "solemn covenant with God" for his people to sign. He proposed it first to the "principal men" of the church, then to "the people" of the neighborhood worship associations he had coaxed into being during the Valley Revival, then publicly to the congregation, and lastly to the deacons for them to "consider." Remarkably, everyone over fourteen years old subscribed to it with their own "hands" and, on a fast day at the meeting house, "solemnly manifested their consent."

The document thanks God for his recent presence, laments the community's "backsliding" and "mountains of sin," and devotes several pages to various pledges. The first pledge covers business transactions. It insists on "rules of honesty, justice, and uprightness" in all dealings; disavows "overreaching" (charging too much) or defrauding; promises to respect property rights; and commits townspeople to consider others' interests "like our own." No one should "injure" a neighbor, and if that should happen, purposely or otherwise, the perpetrator should repair the injury and "remove the offense." Other pledges briefly cover other shortcomings. The final paragraph begs God to "keep us from wickedly dissembling" and "not leave us to our own foolish, wicked, and treacherous hearts." Asking people to sign such a document signified Edwards's near-desperate desire to lock in the Awakening's already meager gains. Naturally it did little good, being, in Perry Miller's sardonic phrase, a "hard oath" for an expanding commercial economy to observe.[95]

The 1742 initiative should in a sense have come as no surprise because Edwards was nothing if not consistent in the matter of charity and wealth. What pains the "wicked" take to "get rich," he preaches in 1722 at age nineteen. They keep "seeking, pulling and drawing, and are never satisfied." Covetous men, though they obtain like Alexander the "whole world," are never satisfied. They commit "theft, fraud and deceit," so that their "money and lands," even if increased, become "cankers" that eat at their substance. How many "accusations of conscience" do they "sin under!"[96] The rich man who fares "sumptuously" and wears "fine apparel" will at last "beg that he may receive a drop of water" from a poor man he looked on in life "as his dog."[97]

And in 1731: "They are not those to whom this ordinance [of the Lord's Supper] is due who have purchased such a blessing with money. They ben't the rich and the worthy" who deserve this, "but the poor, the maimed, the halt and the blind, the naked, the filthy, the miserable, the undone."[98]

And in 1733: "Unjust persons, and those that are fraudulent or oppressive in their dealings," spend their days going to destruction, as do "all covetous persons, that set their hearts chiefly on the riches of this world."[99]

And in 1736: "What great pains and labors" men undertake, "to obtain high degrees of earthly good, that they may excel others, and be above their neighbors in earthly estate, and in honor; that they mayn't make a finer show, and may be in a higher place, and be more accounted for. . . . How great indeed the folly of neglecting [God's things] when we experience within ourselves so great an aptness to be eager after the high things of this vain world, to have a bigger dust heap or dung heap than our neighbors."[100]

And in 1738: God has cursed your fields and sent you wormy crops for not doing "deeds of justice to the poor."[101]

And in 1739: Even saints are "guilty" of sin when they are "without any . . . public charity."[102]

And in 1740: Some families are in such want of bread that they sell nearly anything they have to buy it, yet merchants seize the advantage to raise their prices, thereby extorting money and raising prices for everyone. This is a "violent dealing with our neighbour," an "abominable" type of theft that a man should repair before confronting God's "throne of judgment."[103] Landed families meanwhile think themselves "sorrowfully out" if they "ben't well provided for with food and clothing, or wood to burn, or fodder for their cattle."

And in 1741: Men's "worldliness" and "worldly lusts" for "pleasures and profits and honors" are filling them with pride and undermining "public contributions for pious and charitable uses."[104]

And in 1743: Among a Christian people there ought to be "none" in want—which may require a man with two carts to give one to someone with no cart. The rich, by giving a mere one quarter of their estates, could build houses of worship, schools, or some other public good, but do they? No, because they are "ready through [a] covetous, selfish, close disposition to raise many objections."[105]

And in 1746: "The making a great shew of love, pity, and distress for souls costs 'em nothing; but in order to shew mercy to men's bodies, they must part with money out of their pockets. . . . A true Christian love to our brethren," says Edwards, "extends both to their souls and bodies." He touts the "benevolent, merciful, charitable and beneficent" and in the same breath condemns the "fraudulent" and "oppressive."[106]

Edwards was not hostile to wealth per se or to property or trade or business enterprise. He wanted a safety net and enough redistribution of wealth to meet needs, and commerce that was modulated and regulated by unselfish Christian sensibilities and community values. But he was not an agrarian radical in the mold of early English radicals such as Gerard Winstanley or the Levellers. Personally charitable, as were other members of his family, he was educated, enjoyed a good salary, owned livestock, had well-to-do friends and relatives, and might have lived a life of comfort and even touches of luxury had he permitted himself, which he seldom did.[107] George Marsden calls him (misleadingly, perhaps, for what amounts to a paid public servant in a marginal world who could be terminated at will) an "aristocrat in a hierarchical society that took aristocracy for granted," and Edwards assumed that even the ideal world of Heavenly love to come would show traces of rank and gradation, though of the mind and spirit, not of material wealth.[108]

He was similarly comfortable with rank, order, and gradation in the political realm. Rulers, like God, give direction, rewards, and punishments to the "less knowing, and weaker," a commonplace view in the Atlantic world before the age of revolution that not only accorded in Edwards's mind with Scriptural injunctions—God "loves order"—but, as noted above, reflected the patterns of deference of the mid-eighteenth century.[109] Charity equaled neither political nor socio-economic upheaval, at any rate in Edwards's own time.

Edwards, moreover, readily employed the language of commerce for religious purposes, as did the Scriptural passages on which he drew. He explains Christ's "purchasing" of redemption with his life and how the "price" Christ laid down "pays our debt" and "procures a title." Whoever pays a debt "does in some sense make a purchase, he purchases liberty from that obligation," which is the meaning of Christ's purchase.[110] Christians will enjoy a "vast inheritance," which will be "managed" by God.[111] One drawback to the Valley Revival, he hazards, might have been that people could appear to have run sometimes to the extreme of "too much neglecting their worldly business" and minding nothing but religion.[112]

He appreciates the benefits of trade and exhorts his parishioners to deal honestly in business by fulfilling contracts on time and doing conscientious work when hired to do so, sentiments that conservatives from Daniel Webster to Milton Friedman would have approved. He accepts lending and borrowing for agriculture and trade as a part of economic life and warns more than once, and sometimes at length, that the failure to pay debts would constitute theft, damage the trust needed for trade, and possibly cause (though he did not use these terms) wider defaults.[113] He argues that Scripture does not prohibit usury, which is neither "oppression nor injustice" nor adverse to strangers, and not inconsistent with the "grand command" that is the "second table" of the Mosaic law, "viz. loving our neighbor as ourselves.[114]

Edwards argues, in support of Matthew's phrasing of the Beatitudes ("Blessed are the poor in spirit") rather than Luke's ("Blessed are the poor"), that men of wealth and business can in fact enter Heaven if they conduct themselves as regenerate men laboring for Christ and community. And for all the wickedness he sees in contemporary advances in navigation, he applauds the advances themselves, which facilitate communication and trade and will eventually help usher in the Millennium, a time of "great temporal prosperity."[115] He says during the Great Awakening that true saints will strive, when they see others "grow rich," to pray for, if not their wealth, then at any rate their "happiness," and that people must "improve" their property as best they can, though for God and charity and not simply themselves.[116]

Yet there can be no doubt that Edwards, as his sermons and writings make clear, was at odds with the self-centered materialism and avaricious scheming that seemed to be consuming the Connecticut Valley and the British Empire. He supported private property and trade as spurs to industry and prosperity. But he also feared that unmitigated free enterprise—what George Marsden calls an "individualistic acquisitive modern culture"— would bring out the worst in human nature, and he disapproved, as Robert Jenson says, of the unmodulated "free market mechanism" around him that tempts men with the prospect of accumulation.[117]

Edwards's sermons and writings reflect this fear and disapproval. He inveighs against taking commercial advantage of people's ignorance, of selling defective or overpriced goods, of bargaining that might create real hardship, especially "taking advantage of others' poverty. . . . God will defend their cause and you will be no gainer by such oppression."[118] He accuses men of fraud and deceit, of "leading [others] in the blind" and taking advantage "of their necessities."[119] "Inquire strictly whether or no you have forsaken Mammon" and become, despite your pretenses, "more of a servant of your worldly interest than you are of God."[120] "Men are apt to rely much on their worldly possessions and advantages, and to be much pleased to be themselves so much higher in the world than others. . . . Men's worldly possessions and worldly honour . . . very commonly prove their undoing." Without Christ, this "will prove only to have fatted you for the slaughter."[121] God, after all, commonly gives the blessing of worldly riches to those whom he "despises most."[122] The wicked rich, even if they offer "ten thousand sacrifices to God," cannot buy a path to Heaven.[123] Think seriously about how you bestir yourselves about wood lots or "a market for cattle" or how you pray for good rain and good corn and act as though money and land are a "chief good." Has God "nothing better to bestow . . . than a little money or land?"[124]

Edwards also cannot resist noting that the Millennium's prosperity will come to a fiery end on the Day of Judgment, emphasizing that worldly business is good "no otherwise" than if it moves us toward Heaven; that if a man possesses "money or provisions," it must be solely to "supply him on his journey" to Heaven; that if we "set our hearts on riches and seek happiness in them," death will "blow up all our hopes." Edwards knows that self-interest inevitably "governs the generality of men, who will mind their own interest rather than anything else." He nonetheless insists that they must sacrifice their "private, separate interest to the glory and honor of God and to the public good."[125] And he contrasts the "virtue of generosity" with the "vice of selfishness," the "disposition to prefer self" rather than the "public weal." The "private interest" of a person may be "inconsistent with the public good," may be pursued "in opposition to the public"—which is "base and contemptible" behavior because acting on "selfish principle" will always be "private, narrow and sordid."[126]

Jonathan Edwards never thought that this kind of ideal charitable society would quite materialize here on earth. Enduring charity and love of men depend in the end on enduring love of God, the essence of grace, and grace is unlikely to touch enough depraved souls in a depraved world to carry the day fully and forever. But he could still rely on the traditional weapons for changing human behavior and the human heart—the covenant, the innate conscience, the striving to prepare—and was in any case not one to give up easily. And he issued a kind of standing challenge over the course of his career that he never entirely withdrew. A "worldly spirit" is corrupt. Salvation implies "forsaking the world." Men must sell their all for that "pearl of great price," saving faith. They must, to achieve grace, "sacrifice *every thing*."[127]

❋ 5 ❋
COMMUNITY

*A man is moral when he is social; he is immoral when he is anti-social.
. . . Pride disrupts society. Love equalizes. Humility freely takes its place
as a simple member of the community.*

— WALTER RAUSCHENBUSCH

JONATHAN EDWARDS was a towering minister of the gospel of charity,
but he was equally a towering minister of the gospel of community. The
notion of togetherness—social peace, amiableness, unity, harmony, collective worship, conversation, friendship, neighborliness, holy community, the oneness of mankind—was a major Edwardsian theme, important
for its earthly significance, for its relation to salvation and holiness, and
for the way it foreshadows the realm of Heavenly love, the glorious cul-
mination, in Edwards's view, of the whole of history.

So forceful was Edwards on the need for community, peace, accom-
modation, and togetherness that he may seem at times to undermine
his attack on greed and his demand for charity, both of which involved
criticism, controversy, and potential conflict. He did not. One obvious
goal of charity was to connect those in need to the larger Christian community and those better-off with their poorer brethren. A greater sense of
community would foster greater charity. The need for community arose
in part precisely because of the need for charity. Charity and community
were therefore of a piece, dual expressions of true faith and God's commandment to love thy neighbor and the precepts of the Pauline epistles
on mutual help and brotherly solidarity.

Moreover, community might soften the class tensions and competitiveness that not only made charity necessary but were themselves frag-
menting society. Edwards was no leveler, as we have seen. He considered
inequality not only unavoidable but proper—even the angels in Heaven

have ranks—and he may actually have reinforced a certain species of class antagonism by insisting on the special role of ministers, thereby pitting, as Perry Miller suggests, a group committed to the life of the mind and spirit against those committed to lives of materialism and accumulation. Building a sense of community, besides adhering to Scriptural precept, could conceivably keep these latter tendencies in check.

Miller makes the further interesting point that the New England Puritans were largely lower-middle class within the context of the British Empire because they were not only rustics but Dissenters. Out in the Connecticut River valley, they were in fact, as Christopher Clark indicates, not a lot more than marginal plebeians who were dependent on the patronage of the British establishment but separated from it by a socio-economic chasm. Some were much better off than others, hence the perpetual pulpit bombardment of the wealthy. But preaching unity in this imperial context meant preaching not so much passive acceptance of the status quo as the restraint of the acquisitive self among a people who were, in a certain sense, fundamentally in the same boat. Miller, often considered off target about Edwards, deserves credit for being on target about this.[1]

There were other reasons to stress community. The notion of Christian solidarity touched on sins besides greed and possessiveness, among them the many forms of status seeking and spiritual pride and the petty but destructive habits of gossip, backbiting, and slander—in other words, human as well as capitalist behavior. If charity was important to counteract the mutual antagonisms and imbalances in the economy, community was important to counteract the frictions and abrasions of human beings simply endeavoring to live together in some approximation of harmony. Never mind poverty and competitiveness; it was important to achieve a tolerable level of basic daily amity.

It should further be said that the record of human history and contemporary affairs was for Edwards a telling litany of sin and depravity leading to disunity, strife, and violence among men and nations. This manifestly included colonial America, which had not only a history of internal rebelliousness but a frontier open to foreign attack and an imperial monarchy that, however wise in theory, might in practice strike down the colonial charters and with them religious autonomy. There clearly needed to be local and provincial solidarity to ward off unwarranted incursions from real enemies. Community in this sense was simply prudent public policy.

The quest for community is present in many familiar aspects of Edwards's thought and expression. Thus charity is essential not only for itself but for society. It is, like justice, one of the things whereby "the good of human society [is] maintained and promoted." Charity expresses the pity, compassion, and love that attend saving grace. But it is also "the bond by which the several members of the church of Christ are united" and the act that brings high and low together into Christian community.[2]

Community also figures in Edwards's linguistic tropes and intellectual constructs. It is everywhere, for instance, in the metaphor of sweetness. Sweetness becomes a fountain from which "sweetest" joys spill forth into a community where God is present and there is an "emanation" and "diffusion" of Christ's sweetness. God is the "sweet light of his people"—Christians in their collective identity as his "chosen"—and God will spread himself over his church, the place where his saints gather to enjoy the sweetness of his love and the love in unity to one another.[3] God's presence in the midst of any "people" adds "sweetness and relish" to what they have, as the presence of God's love among the primitive Christians enabled them to eat their meat together with gladness and "singleness of heart."[4] If religion is sweet taken alone, it is even sweeter taken in society, where "communion and mutual communications of pleasure do increase it." Religion "begets love and peace," which "sweetens [men's] conversation and fellowship" and makes people "delight" in one another.[5]

Harmony, the trope conveying relationship, is part and parcel of God, who contains a harmony of proportion and regularity and a disposition or consent—"consentaniety"—as in the "mutual consent and agreement" of diverse things, language redolent of social relations.[6] God in the guise of the Trinity of Father, Son, and Holy Spirit is plural and therefore relational. "One alone cannot be excellent," says Edwards. "If God is excellent, there must be a plurality in God, otherwise, there can be no consent in him." Edwards translates this concept into considerations of the human order and how religion brings harmony to "the society and conversation of men."[7]

Beauty, a synonym in Edwards for excellence and perfection, is the "mutual consent and agreement" of diverse things that evince the fine social features of "order, uniformity [and] harmony."[8] With regard to social relations of different types, when we see "beautiful airs of look and gesture, we naturally think the mind that resides within is beautiful" and possesses "conjointness," Edwards's term for the capacity to join and unite. We observe what affection people have for fellow creatures, and that God contrives for us to feel affection or love for fellow creatures, especially (this being a youthful reflection) "the other sex." The more exalted and beautiful the mind of that person, the more "laudable" the feeling.[9]

As to intellectual constructs, Edwards the young student of physical science sees a universe that, though consisting of many parts, is yet "one," with "one architect" and "one frame" and with the parts having "relation and connection" and "mutual dependence and subserviency," all "sweetly having respect one to another, harmonizing one to another, and orderly united and connected together."[10] "There is a mutual tendency" (à la Newton) "of all bodies to each other," so that gravity preserves the universe, and one part "is hereby beneficial to another. . . . All the well being of the whole frame, depends on it" and represents a "type" of "love or charity" in the spiritual world. It is a short step from the notion of divine multiplicity and consent and a disparate universe of gravitational pull to the idea of human community as "a union of mutual consent" that reflects the orderly connection and dependence of nature.[11]

As a last glance at familiar territory, we may mention truth, not only a touchstone of early Calvinism because it stood in contradistinction to temporal authority but, even more, a self-evident community need. "Union in society is founded in truth," says Edwards. Take that away, "and you destroy all human converse, and there could be no living, nor trading, nor dwelling together." If there be no truth, we are "unfit to be trusted." Especially does truth "become those who not only are united with others in civil society, but in Christian society, in which they are all one body and members one of another."[12] Let us be "plain, free and open one to another" and know "each other's thought," he says, and "walk as children of light."[13]

But community was no mere adjunct to other notions. For Edwards community was a driving force of its own and, like charity, a lifelong preoccupation. One of his earliest sermons, to his first congregation in New

York, was a message of togetherness—communion with Christ, the unity of Christians, the disposition of Christians to "seek and promote each other's good," the good of "the community" as the way to happiness. He thus grinds the powder of community and salvation together from the outset, preaching the eventual "union" of Christ and those who love him, and the prospect of "intimate conversation" with him, and the way to the saintly "conversation" that is our chief pleasure here on earth. We should "do our utmost to forward the salvation of other men," must "lend them a hand" to save their eternal life, must consider our behavior with respect to "justice, charity, beneficence." Still blending salvation and society, he asserts that a Christian's chief goal on earth should be to "do something towards the destruction of the kingdom of Satan, and the setting up of the kingdom of Christ in his own soul *and in the world*."[14]

"Living Peaceably One With Another," a different sermon from the early 1720s, also celebrates Christian community. We are traveling, Edwards says, toward "the region of peace" in the footsteps of "our mild and gentle leader," Jesus Christ, who died for the sake of our peace. Let us therefore (echoing John Winthrop) "bear each other's burdens and bear with each other's infirmities." Let us "pray for each other" and be full of "benevolence, quietness, meekness, and a forgiving temper."

Consider the benefits of peace, he continues, to a "town or society" aspiring to holiness. In a place that is peaceful, the gospel is "like to obtain" and religion "like to flourish." In a place of strife, it will not. "One half of religion consists in peaceableness, in being at peace with our neighbors and brethren," an essential background and logical consequence of the ingathering of souls. All who would see the "kingdom of Christ set up here" (as Edwards clearly does) and their "own souls and the souls of theirs saved" should "follow after peace."

Furthermore, peace "conduces" to the "prosperity of a people." Where peace reigns, people "are ready to advance each other's wealth." Contention, by contrast, destroys every interest in the same way that sins such as covetousness and injustice ruin "wealth." Peace also increases a people's reputation, and according to a people's reputation are they "like to flourish." And it is simply "amiable" to see a society "living together in peace and unity." Therefore let all of us who care about a community's "temporal and spiritual prosperity, its reputation and beauty," do all we can to foster unity: "O, that there may be nothing but perfect amity and agreement!"

But unity is more than just beneficial. It is in our earthly and spiritual DNA, as Edwards explains in this same lovely sermon. "We are all made of the same blood. We are all descendants of the same Heavenly Father who has made us all, and all from the same earthly father and mother; so that we are all brethren, of whatever nation, religion or opinion."[15] We are made to be useful to society, made "one for another" and not for ourselves alone. In fact, we cannot possibly subsist without the help of our fellow men. Unity is therefore God's purpose for us. "God in the creation designed men for society, that we might help each other and love each other; and shall we, instead of that, tear one another or do what tends to make each other's lives uncomfortable?" Since contention and strife are the great destroyers of community peace, we must obviously avoid anything, any behavior, that "tends to contention." Let us rather "follow peace immediately" and everything that "makes for peace."[16]

Edwards elaborated the ideas of blood ties, resemblance to God, and mutual dependence in many works. We are "allied one to another by nature," he preaches in the early 1730s, not long before his 1733 sermon on charity to the poor. "We are made in the image of God," have the "same nature," have "like faculties," similar dispositions, needs, desires of good, and aversion to misery. We are "of one blood," made to "subsist by society and union." God has made us "with such a nature that we can't subsist without the help one of another." People are "as the members of the natural body." They are "One." They cannot survive "alone," without "union."[17]

Men are accordingly "made to live in society and to be useful" to one another. God has given them "such natures and placed them in such a state that they are dependent one on another. . . . We could not live, we could not subsist [if it] were not for the help of others." God saw that men for their "common good" should be "united in society," and that we all have a "debt" to society that we owe for benefits received. Consider our need for other people when we are infants and children or sick or injured or "warding off many things that would tend to destroy us without help." We should therefore "in our turn do them [other people] good," should "employ ourselves for their good," and should in some way "serve human society."[18]

" 'Tis evident," he reiterates, "that man was intended for society." The laws of "nature" and "divine revelation" teach us to be "united with those that we dwell with in the same country, to have a special affection for them, and make us, in many respects, one body with them."[19] "Moral government in a society" is a "social affair," and "the ground of moral behavior is society, or mutual intercourse and social regards."[20] And not only community broadly and abstractly considered but also in the sense of neighbors, comrades, and, in particular, friends. Men have a "natural inclination" to adore a "glorious being infinitely superior," namely God, but also to adore "friendship, to love and delight in a fellow creature . . . that may be conversed with and enjoyed." This is a "natural inclination of ours," our "love and friendship to a companion."[21] And to everyone: "The spirit of piety is a spirit of peace and love" that disposes men to look beyond their "own things." It "unites all parts of the community and strongly cements them together."[22] A people in this "world" have a "general interest" in advancing their "pleasure, profit, peace or honor . . . taken one with another."[23]

The great weight Edwards accorded the concept of community is evident in his occasional observations about colonial politics. Without delving deeply into Edwards's thinking on the question of power, obedience, deference, and governance, a topic demanding its own lengthy study, we may note that he urges leaders to work for "public" prosperity and "public" society. He exhorts them not to fray the "bonds of union" by promoting private interests, and to work instead to make people "subservient to one another's good, which is the end of society."[24] Good leaders are, after all, "members of a community" that God holds dear, and so they too should hold community dear. Godliness should make them "public-spirited," with "respect" to the public, lovers of the "privileges of the people."[25] Edwards condemns leaders, interestingly, mainly for a lack of love for their community rather than for a lack of charity, though since the two usually go hand in hand there is perforce little difference.

Many sermons from the 1720s urge Christians to use collective forms of worship such as public and family prayer, which would become favorite talking points during the Valley Revival, and to cherish close friendships as a way of pursuing collective community ends. "The pleasures of friendship," though not our ultimate goal, surpass all worldly things, he says, though also reassuring parishioners that God himself, especially

in his incarnation as Christ, is likewise a "dear friend." Earthly friendships will, moreover, endure. True, the believer "must leave his friends"
at death, which will be a wrenching moment. But they will likely be re-
stored to one another in Heaven, assuming they are bound by grace, and
so should be cherished all the more on earth.[26]

This was not a mere preoccupation of naive youth. It was a conviction that Edwards sustained over the years. He relished the spirit of togetherness he witnessed during revivals. Although grace is a matter between God and the individual, "community" of the kind Edwards evokes
means, among other things, crowds "pressing" forward toward grace,
with group affections feeding personal affections and spilling over into
evidences of a sanctified community order. One sign of the coming of
the Valley Revival was young people meeting together around town, a
practice their elders soon emulated, thereby producing, Edwards recalls,
"talk" and "conversation" of spiritual and eternal things in "all companies"
and upon all occasions where people gathered. Inhabitants of the town
"thronged" into private houses. There was joy in families and in "public
assemblies." Congregations were alive with "public" worship, concern for
"neighbors," lively "public praises," and multipart collective psalmody.
People discoursed of Christ at weddings, and children formed into religious "societies." Hundreds professed faith, often after hearing "news of
others' conversion." Hundreds took communion.[27]

Salvation is a matter between God and the individual—but within a
social environment. People who experienced their own conversions at
this time expressed a "great desire for the conversion of others," recounts
Edwards, noting that when people are engaged to this extent they will
naturally make it the subject of "conversation when they get together,
in which they will grow more and more free." He searched diligently for
signs of religious conversation and talk because conversation, as he later
writes, is the special "medium" of "union and communication" among
members of society and indeed constitutes the very "being of society as
such."[28] When people converse about religion and salvation, there will
naturally be additional manifestations of piety such as "outward prayer,
singing psalms, going to the public assemblies of God's people, attending the sacraments, keeping days of fasting or thanksgiving, reading and
hearing the word of God, attending private religious meetings, speaking

respectfully of God, talking much of God and Christ, and seeming affectionate and reverential in the manner of our talk of things of religion or in our manner of behavior" in worship.[29]

People in 1735, he says, seemed "united" in love and affection for one another and "all mankind," including even "enemies" and the "meanest of mankind" or an "Indian in the woods."[30] Even when the revival spirit flagged after 1735, the "religious conversation," private "religious meetings," and "meetings on Sabbath-nights" continued, wrote Edwards, and the Great Awakening a few years later renewed this sort of collective holiness.[31] There was a more charitable spirit toward the poor, and more religious conversation and prayer and social worship in the neighborhood societies that he had previously organized. The sermons of George Whitefield melted the "whole assembly of the congregation," and still greater numbers "conversed" about religion and met for pious purposes, including young people and children who "talked together." There were sermons to "companies" in private homes that propagated affection "throughout the room," and people from other parts of town would arrive and try to get in the door. Edwards met in his own home with groups of young people who were "most affected" with "humility, self-condemnation, self-abhorrence, love, and joy," all vital visible elements of holy community. After public exercises ended at the meeting house, people would remain in "conference" and in group prayer and song, and conversions arose more frequently "in the presence of others, at religious meetings . . . under public observation."[32]

We see Edwards during the Awakening direct parishioners to study Christ's Sermon on the Mount and the Book of James ("love thy neighbor as thyself") for lessons on duties to others—far superior steps toward holiness, he insists, than mere external habits of worship or acts of self-denial such as fasting. The united family of saints becomes a template for a pious community in the same way, he believes, that Christ made the disciples "his family." He emphasizes that we need "the help and society of friends," and hopes to see flourishing "companies," "societies," and "families" of Christians.[33] He reiterates the importance of religious "conversation" and "talk," which indicate Christian sociability and "solemnize the hearts of natural men." He tells his congregants that for God to dwell here they must be "united" in, for example, "public assemblies" and at "the Lord's table." He invokes God's covenant with New England to encourage, in Harry Stout's phrase, "a *collective* rededication" to holiness, and produces to that end the famous written covenant of 1742 for townspeople to sign.[34]

Edwards also expands his horizons far beyond the Connecticut Valley and New England, as might be expected of a citizen of the British Empire and an active participant in the "republic of letters." He argues in the 1740s, as he had in the 1720s, that the "world of mankind" scattered across the "face of the earth" are "one blood," and he insists, as he had as a young pastor, that performing our moral duties means doing good not only to our kinsmen, neighbors, and fellow colonists but also to "men" and "mankind."[35] The whole "gospel-dispensation" of Christ's time, he insists, aimed to "abolish the enmity, and break down the partition-wall between Jews and Gentiles, and of twain to make one new man," and so make "peace" and annihilate "all disposition in nations and particular persons to despise one another," and to "establish the contrary principles of humility, mutual esteem, honor and love, and universal union."[36] Edwards was clearly trying to do his part, through revivals, argumentation, letters, and the encouragement of missionaries such as David Brainerd, to further this expanded cause.

Edwards was the chief American proponent of the so-called Concert of Prayer, a plan developed by Scottish ministers in the mid-1740s to organize simultaneous global prayer meetings that might hasten the advent of the "glorious day" of the Spirit that would blaze a path to the pre-Apocalyptic Millennium, when there would be a true worship of God among his "visible people" and the turning of "multitudes" from idolatry. The language he uses to describe this effort partially reprises the language of his early ministerial days. There would be not only solitary prayer but private group praying and "public meetings," moments of maximum "unity" in "congregations, families and other praying societies" all spurred by the thought of "multitudes" doing likewise throughout the (Protestant) world. The times for group prayer would emerge from "friendly, harmonious" habits of local "conversation," and this "disposition" to prayer and "union" would spread, in the familiar dynamic of revivalism, to the "awakening of others" until it reached the "highest stations" and "whole nations" to form a "visible union" and bring about the long reign of

"Christ's kingdom" on earth. "They who shall be united" are the people of "many cities" (from Zachariah) and "many countries" who have agreed "unitedly" to pray for this blessed end.[37]

The means are familiar, but the result that Edwards anticipated, the hastening toward the early days of the Millennium, though something he had always anticipated, prompted at this late stage of his career not just social and communitarian but utopian rhetoric. It will be a time, Edwards argues in *An Humble Attempt To promote Extraordinary Prayer,* when the poor will rise from the dust and beggars from the dung, and the exalted will be holy. All heresy and superstition will vanish, and the earth shall be "united as one holy city, one Heavenly family." There will be not only wonderful union but the most universal peace, love, and (tropes abounding) "sweet harmony," when men of all nations will "sweetly correspond one with another as brethren and children of the same father" and the "great society" shall appear in "glorious beauty." A civil union, a "harmonious agreement among men in the management of their secular concerns," is "amiable," he says, but "much more a pious union, and sweet agreement in the great business for which man was created." Surely, he pleads, this is "worth *praying* for."[38]

The "Concert" went more or less nowhere even in Northampton, but the way Edwards wrote about it reveals something of the intensity and breadth of his long-standing disposition toward holy society. This would find its way into his stark mid-century treatise *The Great Christian Doctrine of Original Sin.* The gospel aims, he writes here, to break down walls, make "one new man," and bring a time of "universal union" and peace when, he then argues, the "poor famishing wretch" will come to a "glorious feast" at the table of God, the only potentate, and "she" that was "friendless, forsaken, and desolate" will enter "eternal espousals" with Christ.[39] Edwards's concern for the social is also present in *The Nature of True Virtue,* a mid-century treatise that explores how the regenerate heart's love for God transforms a natural man's "base" private virtue, his "sordid" and "contemptible" self-love, into a "complex" virtue that enables him to act for the public good and the "public weal," touchstones of a holy society progressing on the path to Heaven.[40]

Edwards never surrendered the notion, says Clyde Holbrook, that the final end of man was "social . . . whether in history or beyond history."[41] He exalted virtue, says E. Brooks Holifield, because it generated "social harmony" and a humble consent to God's power and love.[42] We cannot separate Edwards building Christ's kingdom in men's souls, says Paul Ramsey, from Edwards building the kingdom "in the world among men."[43] He believed, says Willem van Vlastuin, in "the power of the Spirit" to renew "hearts, characters, families, churches, and society."[44] As Edwards himself puts it, a person's duty is to promote "God's glory, *and* the good of mankind" as the "very business" of life.[45]

Edwards used language to assail sins against community that matched the language he used to assail miserliness and lack of charity. Chief among his targets are "strife and contention," the companions of "enmity . . . contempt [and] quarreling."[46] "Strife and contention, malice, and mutual ill" bear a "great and universal dominion amongst mankind." They are "some of the greatest miseries of this apostate world" because in them we see men who are made "of the same blood" and are from the same first father and mother "devour, malign and persecute one another, and with heart and hand work out one another's misery." They allow "ambition, and avarice, and self-seeking, and treachery" to smother piety with the "spirit of contention."[47] People who should work for the "public good" fall prey to "strife and contention," "jealousies and envyings." They become corrupt and produce enmity, and the strength and wealth of a place are consumed by "the ambition and avarice of men in its own bowels."[48]

Men are not happier for being possessed of "pride, malice, revenge" and other such sins against God and man, argues Edwards, ever a shrewd analyst of psychological states.[49] Instead, they feel bitter, are "fierce against those that oppose and dislike 'em," are "proud, malicious, invidious, and revengeful," which feeds their discontent and unhappiness. Some are so consumed with "pride, ambition, malice, hatred, revenge, and deceit" that they form what Edwards calls "parties," groupings of people with similar personal likes and dislikes, to which they become implacably "knit."[50] They pretend they don't "hate their enemies, but they really do in their hearts."[51] They know the "old leaven of malice." They drown themselves in "contention."[52]

Edwards ascribes some of this behavior to environmental factors, noting correctly that in the grip of sloth, boredom, and sometimes alcohol over the course of the long New England winter, people sink into gossip. They express "jealousies" and "evil surmises" with no basis, "speak evil" to or of men, "show a spirit against neighbors," threaten others with "unruly tongues—and thus put a "family" or a "town" into a "fire of contention." Strife feeds "evil speaking" and "backbiting" and whispering of the "ill things" a neighbor has done. There are "plottings and contrivings," "lying [and] slandering," "false reports," and "fraudulent, knavish, vile" accusations. Contention is a many-layered evil for Edwards. It harms the work of building holy community because it disturbs men's own hearts. It distracts people from religious devotion. It injures trust—the "truth" necessary for binding society. It destroys society's "comfort" and "beauty" by creating "confusion" and confounding "good order."[53] Where there is "envying and strife," there is "confusion and every evil."[54]

Two particular sins are contention's "root and spring": envy and pride.[55] It is difficult to know which Edwards found more offensive, envy or pride, since they were so frequently intertwined, but when he paired them, as he often did, envy usually came first. Envy gives rise to contention, he says in "Envious Men," a fierce sermon from 1730, simply because (as we would expect Edwards to argue) it is a derivative of the lust for possessions, of a man's drive to compare his wealth, or his success in accumulating wealth, to someone else's. Envy is a man feeling "grieved or uneasy [at] another's prosperity" or experiencing an "uneasiness" or "hurt" at the honor or wealth" of other men. It is invidious, in a word, therefore social: "When another's prosperity be grievous, that is envy."[56]

The nature of this kind of materialistic secular envy is tricky in Edwards because it reflects not only the perspectives of different economic strata but different trajectories within the economy. Some envy others, as might be expected, because others' "prosperity is greater," and they "can't bear" to see others "above them." But Edwards is a near-Veblenian observer of covetous behavior, and he notes that a man may also envy someone "whose prosperity is not so great as his own," yet is approaching "too near an equality" to tolerate. He wants to be "higher above his neighbor" than he is. This is a criticism of the perversely envious attitudes of the already prosperous toward the almost prosperous rather than criticism of lesser fry envying the lofty. Comparative rates of accumulation are a factor, too. "Ben't you grieved," Edwards asks, at your neighbors' prosperity and "hurt in your spirit" that they have "such advantages to get money," that they get it so easily and "grow rich so fast" and so much "easier and faster" than you? "How impertinent" that you feel "hurt" because another prospers! How "silly" to "distress" yourself if someone else "gets money apace."[57]

Less urgent but still significant is envy of honors and influence. Men grieve that another "is put into office" and "grows great." "Ben't you hurt" when someone has "much power and influence" so that you desire to pull him down? Don't you justify your criticisms, in public and to yourself, on the grounds of patriotism or justice or worthiness, even though in reality "'tis the person's honor or prosperity" itself that prompts your concern? Be honest. Are there not "old grudges" and a "spirit of revenge" for ancient affronts? Consider all this carefully, says Edwards, because "particular men" do the most in "maintaining a party spirit." They are "hottest with hatred, wrath, and strife, and envy" and "blow up the same flame in others," thus becoming instruments for "bringing contention into a society" and ringing a death knell for prospects for a community of Christians and mankind.[58]

The castigation of envy reaches a kind of pinnacle in *Charity and Its Fruits,* the long sermon series of 1738. Here Edwards condemns on now-familiar grounds the "malignant, malicious spirit" that envies others' "comparative happiness" and hates the prosperity of those above them or who might soon rival them or who enjoy spiritual standing or worldly honors. Is there not, Edwards says as he had said in 1730, a terrible unease at our neighbors' success and a desire to see them "brought down?" Do we not spend too much of our lives "with envy burning in our hearts towards one another," thus sowing division, contention, and strife? Do we not seethe with an immoderate, unquenchable anger that debilitates us, our church, and our community?[59]

Wicked though envy is, pride is at least as wicked. Pride was at the center of Edwards's perennial battles against Arminianism, which claimed that men could affect their own salvation, the very idea of which diminished the majesty of God: "Pride is [an] obstacle to the entering of divine light."[60] And pride is of course absolutely ubiquitous, a standing danger to the individual and to society. Edwards tries to convey pride's iniquity by bundling this sin with other sins. The "pride" of the wicked shows in

their "covetousness, malice, envy and revenge."[61] Satan builds his kingdom on the double foundations of "pride and worldliness," "pride and
worldlymindedness," forming great obstacles to receiving and acting on
the gospel.[62] Pride is self-love, which generally implies "revenge" and "hatred."[63] The saints themselves wallow in pride when they show the fatal
telltale signs—malice, revenge, "drunkenness," "fraud," "deceit," "theft,"
and "covetousness." When they do, they destroy their own contentment,
for "pride and self-conceit" leave little room for the modesty that leads
to peace.[64]

Edwards's language could be sulfurous. "You," the congregation, are
nothing but proto-Arminians—"poor, worthless, vile, polluted worms
of dust, yet so arrogant" as to "think yourself sufficient" to displace
Christ and order the "great affairs of the world." Such "self-righteousness" is nothing but "pride and vanity," "hypocrisy and filthiness." What
a figure "you, a poor worm," would make if you should try to stand in
God's stead. This would be self-righteous "folly," "wild and extreme." It
would bring out the evils of "contention" and the spirit of "malice." It
would generate attitudes of "pride" and "irreverence," "disobedience,"
and "self-sufficiency." It would produce, as it did in ancient times with
the children of Israel, a failure to sacrifice that would be an invitation
to ruin.[65]

Pride and self-love are not quite the same for Edwards. Pride is "diverse
from self-love, as we use the word [to mean] a selfish love." But they are
close. Self-love of this kind invariably "includes pride and worldliness
both," which it must, argues Edwards, because pride is fundamentally
social. It is comparative and invidious, an individual's longing to be perceived as superior to others—a dynamic that is social by its very nature.
"Pride is that habit or state of a person's heart whereby he is inordinately
disposed to exaltation amongst other beings as to his comparative dignity,
or worthiness of esteem and value." It has "no consideration of excellence
as such, or of "loveliness or desirableness" in their "own nature." It is a
"comparative dignity that pride affects," a preoccupation with "the light
that one is in or may be conceived to be in amongst other beings."

Pride is therefore a social evil. It is not a desire to enjoy the "love and
esteem of others absolutely," that is, for innate qualities. It is about "comparative esteem and value. It don't content pride" to be valued intrinsi-

cally. " 'Tis a person's comparative exaltation ... that is the proper and immediate object of pride"—not whether a person *is* "above his inferiors, or higher than his equals, or above or equal or nearer to his superiors," but whether he is *seen* to be. Its object is to appear "high amongst them, sufficient without them, independent [of] them," to be "ostentatious, and make a show of one's own dignity to others, to expect respect and honor from others," to "detract from them, to despite [despise] them," to "treat them with contempt, or at least to deny'em that honor and respect," whether they are above or below, "that belongs to them." It is a "habit or state of a person's heart whereby he is thus inordinately disposed to his own exaltation, [or] self-conceit, or an inordinate high thought of self."[66]

Pride signals a confidence in one's "self-sufficiency" and ability to live without others, a "leaning" to one's own "understanding and self-exalting."[67] It is a sin of the heart that is "contrary to Christ," a "*pride,* or an inordinate affecting of [one's] own comparative dignity or ... disposition to self-exaltation," a disposition to affect our own "comparative dignity," a "proud haughty conceit" such as "boasting."[68] Pride is the enemy of holiness because it exalts the individual and denigrates God. And because proud individuals distance and separate themselves from the rest of the social order and breed envy and malice, it is also the enemy of community.

Pride for Edwards naturally included covetousness. "What revenge and malice," he scolds, "what covetousness," how much "spirit of pride has appeared in you!"[69] You show "pride and vanity," strive for a "flaunting appearance" in "buildings and apparel and way of living," care about "outward ornaments" rather than the ornaments of the mind. "How indefatigable are men in endeavoring to increase their estates, to grow rich and great?" How many "unjust things" and little "tricks to deceive" and habits of "oppression" occur "for the sake of worldly gain?" Scripture reproves any kind of pride—in "wit," in "high and honorable stations," especially in "riches."[70] A "selfish proud man," far from selling "all for Christ," cares "nothing for others" and "calls lovely [only] what contributes to his interest" and "ambition."[71]

Material pride is thus a seedbed for contention and strife, which are the great enemies of community, "the spirit and condemnation of the devil." Some of you have "vaunted yourselves in your apparel! Others in their riches! Others in their knowledge and abilities! . . . And how [you] have shown your pride by setting up your wills, and in opposing others, and stirring up and promoting division, and a party spirit in public affairs!"[72] Pride engenders insecurity and "dishonesty in business," so that we see people "running so far into debt" that they will "live above their estates" no matter how secure or elevated or wealthy they appear to be. Many in fact find themselves living so loftily "upon so small a foundation that they never are like to be able to pay their debts." They go "far beyond their condition, or what would be suitable for them" given their actual income, and so are doomed from their "manner of living" to be "always far behindhand." They ultimately "live upon their neighbors"—which, if it results from over-consumption rather than misfortune, is for Edwards a sin.[73]

Even when secular, pride is of course not wholly pecuniary. As already noted, learning and honorific positions engender pride, as do "abilities" and "wit." And this, like naked greed, rends the social fabric as men jostle for status and place. People seek knowledge to be "accounted to know more than others, and to see further," think nothing "more ignominious and disgraceful" than to be a fool, endeavor to "look down upon poor ignorant persons as beneath them and unworthy to stand in equality with them."[74] In 1750 Edwards, who had seen much by now of the world, makes the following perceptive observation about ambition and its complicated consequences. "Men assume power and authority which don't belong to'em." This "provokes" authority and is what men of power "will not bear." Both those in authority and those who challenge them "exalt themselves in their pride . . . [and] assume to themselves God's prerogatives." They have "set themselves highest," he accuses, reaching back to the language of the meeting house controversy. They "take the first seat."[75]

There is no doubt that Edwards chastises the challengers of social rank and elite politics for promoting contention, noting that "a proud spirit is a rebellious spirit" and that "a servant who is of a haughty spirit, is not apt in everything to be submissive and obedient."[76] In this respect he tends to endorse the existing social hierarchy. But he also addresses members of the elite who are "provoked" by and resent their challengers and can't stand acts of "pride and arrogance" toward themselves. Pride exercised "one towards another" in this way "is a thing very abominable." People "cannot endure" it. Men who are "much above others by birth or by the place they stand in, or the authority they are vested with" resent it if their inferiors "treat them with slight and disregard," which thereby fuels the fires of strife.

Edwards chastises the pride and envy of all worldly status aspirations, from whatever social quarter, as a threat to unity and peace. Witness, he repeats long after the fact, the rending of the social fabric during the pew struggle when men trumpeting wealth alone manifested "an arrogant spirit . . . to assume to themselves the rights of others . . . and jostle others out of their places" for a "higher seat in the meeting house."[77]

Christianity is the true way out of this unhappy state. But that raises the problem of spiritual pride, a youthful concern of Edwards that loomed larger during the revivals, where he detects, to his dismay, "spiritual pride's workings," a censorious "condemning" of others, an "unsuitable boldness and confidence." This is "self-righteousness," the "spirit of pride" which tends to a "principle or disposition" to be proud of our own "supposed righteousness, or moral dignity."[78] Spiritual pride is a "hateful lust." It leads people "to think they don't need [spiritual] instruction," which "adds fierceness and bitterness to zeal" by removing the guiding hand of the minister.[79] True zeal is not "proud" and "ostentatious," "rash and inconsiderate," full of "self-exalting" and "superstitious" practices such as pretending to direct revelation. True zealots don't "fiercely" oppose evil or "set themselves off as much better" than others or act from a "proud conceit" of their own judgment. Judgmental zeal of this kind is in fact nothing but a gushing "fount of pride," "most hot and fierce" in men who are themselves "proudest"—"Pharisees" or "proud, persecuting, Romish clergy."[80] Anyone who judges and censures is usually himself a "very proud man."[81]

Christian zeal requires, instead, a "depression" of the self because true Christianity is "attended with humility."[82] Christians must be "humbled for sin" and have a "broken heart and a contrite spirit," a "broken" and a "pure" heart. This is a formulation, drawn from Scripture, that allows Edwards to link secular and spiritual pride. Just as "worldlimindedness . . . stand[s] in the way" of one, the pure of heart, so "self-righteousness" thwarts the other, the contrite and broken of heart. Forsake not only "carnal things," Edwards exhorts, but also the "self-righteous disposition" that turns even self-denial into pride. And be genuine about it. Otherwise you might become like the Jews who mortified their flesh by placing weights on their heads, thorns on their robes, stones on their hard beds, and cords around their waists, taking much "pleasure in thinking how much better they are than others" in performing these rites, and therefore how much more worthy to "sit in the chief places in the synagogues."[83] Or else you might become like "anchorites and recluses" who are so possessed of the "Moloch of spiritual pride" that they "don't renounce their own dignity and righteousness."[84]

Don't be "presumptuous," he warns. "No corruption is so apt to work as pride," especially when it comes in the "disguise of great humility." It is the sin of "devils," the "chief root," he says in 1741, of the false and divisive "extravagance we have lately seen." Forsake pride, or you will "never come to be truly humbled" and will experience neither grace nor peace, for the unregenerate have a "vicious self-love" and "evil inclinations of the will" and stand ready to "entertain a spirit of revenge," the bane of all human society.[85]

Yet Edwards evoked the beauties of community as easily as he condemned the strife that threatened it. He urges a peace where people are "united as brethren" and devoted "with one heart" to seeking "the good of one another and the community."[86] He urges obedience to true Christian values and behavior as revealed in the word and works of God, who will "advance" and "dwell with him who's humble and contrite."[87] For the good of the world as well as the soul, we should feel a "humble, amiable disposition," know a "meek and forgiving spirit and practice," experience the "spiritual and abasing" quality of our faith. We should not only do good works, mortify our lusts, and keep God's commandments. We should also eschew strife by "bridling our tongues" and "selling all for Christ." We should feel "humility, a broken and contrite heart," become "poor in spirit," disclaim "all worthiness and glory."[88]

We should, in other words, live by "the genius of the gospel of peace" and hold fast to a "peaceable spirit, or a spirit of Christian meekness and calmness" even when we are engaged in "Christian warfare" against sin or running the "Christian race" toward grace. "A meek and quiet spirit" is the proper means to victory. Meekness is of "great price" in the sight of God."[89]

We should in fact study and practice the virtues of Jesus Christ, which in Edwards's reading were social as well as spiritual. We should absorb and practice, for example, Christ's "sweet benevolence," his "benignity," "sweet grace and bounty," "glory and goodness," "mildness and gentleness."[90] We should observe Christ's "love and friendship to his disciples" and his concern to comfort his disciples more than himself. We should dwell on his "pitiful and compassionate nature," on the "tenderness of his heart and his great love to mankind," and on his goodness, love and "condescension," or willingness to lower himself to our level. Christ avoided the pitfalls of pride and strife, says Edwards. He was never tempted to "feign" agony in death for "honor and applause." He never sought to be "revenged of his enemies" or counseled his disciples to seek revenge. He counseled them on the contrary to treat all men with compassion. He washed the feet of Judas and others not out of pride but because he was "wonderfully meek."

Jesus, the very son of God, did not seek "promotion and advancement," court men's favor, or appear "ostentatious or forward." He showed contempt for the honors and "glory of the world," flattered neither "small nor great to get honor." He showed not pride but "humility" and a "charitable beneficent spirit," a "mildness" and "self-denial," a steadfast "obedience and trust." Ever "kind, gentle, compassionate and condescending" and of "warm, lively and tender affections," Jesus was willing to eat and drink with "publicans and sinners" and was unwilling to "despise the gentiles."[91] His life illustrates "wonderful instances of humility" and love to God and "astonishing instances of condescension, humility, meekness, lowliness, love to men, love to his enemies, charity, and patience." When we imitate Christ in these things, "then are we holy, and not till then."[92]

Many of the quotations in the three previous paragraphs are from the 1720s, a decade when Edwards might, some speculate, have been more hopeful than he was later about the likelihood of grace abounding and holy community. But he actually sounds not much different a decade later when he praises the Valley Revival for its "spirit of meekness, modesty, self-diffidence," for persons appearing "so ready to think others better than themselves," for the widespread "exercise of resignation to God, and humble submission to his will."[93] Or when he writes, in his notebooks from that decade, of Christ as an example of "submission, humility, meekness, and patience" in remaining "most humble" despite the temptation to become proud, and of Christ's "calmness of spirit," "composure and quietness," "forgiveness," and "patience" and "contempt" for the glory of the world.[94] Or during the Great Awakening: "'Tis best" not to boast of your "great things" or favors from God or your worthiness to "speak before kings." Keep a "very humble manner" lest you arouse resentment and envy, the progenitors of strife, in those who may be watching. Remember how Christ admonished even the disciples for petty jealousy when Mary, sister of Lazarus, anointed him with precious oil from a precious pure-white alabaster box.[95]

Religious Affections, his famous treatise of 1746, maintains in the same vein that true Christians should be of a "serious, religious, devout, humble, meek, forgiving, peaceful, respectful, condescending, benevolent, merciful, charitable and beneficent walk and conversation"—precisely the virtues of Jesus Christ that will lead us toward community. Christ's "wisdom from above" is "pure." It is "peaceable, gentle, easy to be entreated, full of mercy." It is full of "humility, meekness, love, forgiveness, and mercy," full of the "great Christian duty of self-denial" and the Christian "character" that brings us to "God and one another." Soldiers of Christ, insists Edwards, must maintain a "holy calm, meekness, sweetness, and benevolence" amidst "storms" and "injuries." Christian fortitude consists in "ruling and suppressing the evil and unruly passions and affections of the mind" with "good affections." Christ did not demonstrate his "holy boldness and valor" by "fiery passions" or "fierce and violent speeches and vehemently declaiming" against adversaries. He did not show valor by "opening his mouth" or shedding others' blood but by praying that his Father would forgive his enemies and by "going as a lamb or a sheep" with "patience, meekness, love, and forgiveness," with a "dovelike spirit"—with the "humility, quietness, and gentleness of a lamb, and the harmlessness, and love, and sweetness of a dove."[96]

Edwards drew on examples from history for insights into the virtues that make community. Abraham showed "kindness and respect" even to Sodom and other "cities of the plain," demonstrating that those who dwell with a "wicked people" still "become one body" with them as with a brother.[97] David, while fighting for the deliverance and safety of Israel, prayed against his enemies but only as public enemies of God's people rather than as private persons, and he deserves praise for bringing "the whole body of the people" into "exact and beautiful order."[98] Solomon, whose name signifies "peace," was not only the son of a woman once married to a Gentile but a unifier of his people and a "type" of the Messiah. Noah's ark gathered creatures "tame and wild, gentle and rapacious, innocent and venomous," all of whom dwelt in peace.[99]

Edwards harks at times to the Puritan "fathers" who "went after God" in the wilderness and created a land of "love" and "religion" that spread "amongst rulers and ministers and heads of families."[100] He also read British eighteenth-century moral philosophy, much of which touted a politics that assumed innate sociability, trustworthiness, and habits of politeness, and while he apparently read partly in order to refute, reading of this sort might have exerted some influence on his thinking about the possible unity of humanity.[101]

But Jonathan Edwards was above all a preacher of the gospel, in this case the gospel of community. And as with charity, incomparably the most powerful example for himself and others was always the life and message of Jesus Christ. Christ held the keys to community as he did to charity. In the late 1740s Edwards drew up a long list of Christ's virtues as revealed in Scripture. Christ, we read, was not proud, sought no glory or special assistance. He did not set himself above the Law and the Prophets or affect to presume authority or make a show of holiness or fasting or miracles. He flattered neither "small nor great." He "tended to prevent" the rich from following him and refused to promise worldly prosperity to his followers. He also showed immense personal warmth—mildness, humility, and meekness; moderation, calm, and forgiveness; liveliness and tenderness; condescension to children and "the mean" and "satisfaction in union and communion with them." He showed compassion and a loving temper and kind manner. He was gentle and loving to his disciples, was steadfast and cheerful in doing God's will, was willing to pay tribute to Rome to avoid offense, was content to do without the "respect and society of the great," was patient and self-denying in the face of "Satan's temptation" and insults.[102]

The virtues of Christ, studied with care, as Edwards urged, are the virtues of holy community. Edwards was a communitarian for the simple reason that he was a Christian. This is evident in a passage from *Religious Affections* that exudes a rhetorical power rare even for Jonathan Edwards, that fairly glows with passion for the social virtues, and that seems a fit conclusion to this chapter. We will most readily discover the signs of true salvation, he says, in "love to God" and in "love to men" and "saints" and "enemies," in "meekness and forgiveness" and "mercy and charity," in "doing good to men's souls and bodies" and to "particular persons and to the public," in "temperance" and "humility" and in "bridling the tongue" and showing "kindness"—in walking "as Christians in all places, and at all seasons, in the house of God, and in their families, and among their neighbors, on Sabbath days, and every day, in business and in conversation, towards friends and enemies, towards superiors, inferiors and equals ... for God and Christ, and the interest of religion, and the benefit of their brethren," and with the "sweet odor of Christian graces and Heavenly dispositions."[103]

This—the creation of true community—is the *sole* reliable evidence of rebirth.

❄ **6** ❄

LOVE

Unenforceable obligations are beyond the reach of the laws of society. They concern inner attitudes, genuine person-to-person relations, and expressions of compassion which law books cannot regulate and jails cannot rectify. . . . Man-made laws assure justice, but a higher law produces love.

— MARTIN LUTHER KING JR.

LOVE PERVADES Jonathan Edwards's ministry and writings, a point often overlooked given his lingering reputation as a preacher of damnation. In fact, Edwards, though understanding, as we have seen, that fear had its utility in the pulpit, was overwhelmingly a minister of the gospel of love rather than of fear. The doctrine of Christian love ("God is love," "God so loved the world," "the greatest of these is love") achieved its fullest expression in the gospel and epistles of John and the letters of Paul, and Edwards referenced these books thousands of times over the course of his ministry and built some of his greatest sermons around them, weaving love's power and urgency into the fabric of his ministry to a degree that stands out even in comparison to other great figures of the cloth and cloister. Though a Calvinist, Edwards was not chiefly a preacher of damnation. Though damnation was ever at hand, Edwards the Calvinist was chiefly a preacher within the tradition of Christian love. Considering Edwards in this context will locate him at the epicenter of his faith and increase our understanding of what he was about.

Love saturates Edwards's theology and his ideas about holiness and holy society—what Paul Ramsey calls the "Christian moral life," which encompasses charity and community and sainthood and Heaven and cannot be fully grasped without attention to love.[1] True religion, says Ed-

98

wards, is "summarily comprehended in love."[2] The Edwardsian God is an awesome entity whose absolute power Edwards spent his life explaining and defending against the lax, the misguided, and the skeptical. But he is more than powerful. He is also absolutely perfect, beautiful, and excellent and therefore, in Edwards's scheme of things, he loves himself and his own beauty and perfection and excellence. God embodies the essence of "love" and the "act of love" because he has an "infinite . . . love of himself" and his own "beauty." He loves himself with a "holiness" and "delight" that match his own excellence.[3] "Delight in himself" is the sum of God's "inclination, love and joy."[4] God's "nature and temper" are love.[5]

Love swirls as well through Edwards's conception of the Trinity, a vital component of his theology, because for there to be genuine love there must be others to love. This is true even for God, who loves himself but does so within the context of a tripartite Godhead comprising God the father, his son Christ, and the Holy Spirit, each with a particular theological identity and function, each remaining nonetheless a part of the composite whole. Love is therefore an attribute of God and also of the Trinitarian Godhead, whose "divine nature and essence" and "holiness and happiness" consist and subsist in the "perfect and intimate" love between Father and Son and Holy Spirit in a "bond" of full "union." The happiness of the Deity, "as all other true happiness," consists in "love and society." The Trinity constitutes the society that allows God's love to express itself. God's joy is a "social happiness" in the persons of the Trinity.[6] Love is therefore inherently and irreducibly social and relational.

God, moreover, loves perfection so much that he created the world and its creatures, humans included, out of a joyous exuberant desire to expand and radiate himself into infinity. God's love to himself, his "disposition . . . to communicate" and "diffuse his own good[ness]," constitutes "a love to whatever is worthy and excellent," and his "love to himself" is nothing but "delight" in excellence.[7] God inevitably loves all his creation, which is only himself writ large, and therefore loves men because they, like all else, are his creations. However, humans are also special. God loves humans because they are his "children," his "creatures" (creations), but he also loves them because they are "in his image" and "partake of his loveliness" and therefore possess spiritual and intellectual capacities that are comparable, even though inferior, to those of God himself—including, notably, the capacity not only to hold God in awe but to love him as he loves them.[8]

God's creation of the universe as an act of love for himself is also an act that allows for an "increasing communication of himself" to humanity. This allows humans to enjoy an "increasing knowledge of God" and "love to him" and "joy in him," so that God and man may share the dual affections of love and joy. Persons may therefore possess a "heart of love" that draws "nearer to God." They may become "one with God," may be "confirmed to God" in an absolute "identity" and "union."[9] "Love's dwelling in us" is evidence of "the Spirit of God dwelling in us."[10]

God's "love to us and our love to him," says Edwards, reaching into his supply of metaphors, "are in their fountain the same," which works divine love deeply into human relations. God's love to us is a fountain "flowing out to us, and our love to God is only something communicated from that fountain to our hearts." Our love for the deity, our love of "God's nature," is the chief of all affections, a feeling that may build at times into passion and become a "fountain of all other affections," including affection to all humans. God's love, Edwards says, shifting tropes, is a mighty base, the "lowest foundation" and common denominator of the saints' love to the Deity, the foundation of "all the affections" that come afterwards, including the affections of man to man. "Knowledge of [divine] loveliness" is thus "the proper foundation" of such love, an outward expansion of an "inward soul-ravishing sense of mutual love between God and us."[11]

Love is Christ-centered as well as God-centered. God loves people, as is evident from the way he showers them with "grace and love." But he loves them also because of the willingness of his own son and incarnation, Jesus Christ the redeemer, to love them enough to suffer and die for them, thus winning—"purchasing"—God's affection. He purchased "God's love, favor and delight" for us and hence our capacity for "communion with God." Christ's death was the greatest of all acts of love, an expression of the "love which is between the Father and the Son," an "infinitely sweet energy." In addition, Jesus Christ enabled men to more fully apprehend and adore God and to identify and unite with him because they were able to adore and identify with his incarnation, Christ. Christ "drew men to him," says Edwards, so that the Spirit of God, "which is love," could produce a "holy amorous disposition"—a love between Christ and men and the saints of his church as intense as the "virtuous and pious and pure love between a man and his spouse."[12]

When we "delight at the thought of God's loving us" but cannot, given the overwhelming fact of God's majesty, quite "conceive of that love," we have our "passionate love of Christ" to cling to and are able in this way to form a "union with the divine nature."[13] The union between God the Father and Christ the Son thus extends to all, who become "one with God, united with him, centering most perfectly in him." We are "swallowed up in him" in the manner of Christ.[14] People are therefore able to love God for two reasons—because of God's manifest excellence and perfection, and because they can embrace and identify with God's lovely human incarnation, Jesus Christ.

This ability of humanity to love God is vital for Edwards. Among other things, it legitimates the demand that even the unregenerate should express an outward love of God, whether or not they actually feel it. Anyone who does not is surely obtuse if not wicked. " 'Tis the duty of a man that is without those things that essentially belong to love," namely grace and regeneration, to "love God" anyway, since it is an "indispensable obligation that lies on all men at all times, and in all circumstances."[15] God is to be "loved and honored" because he is "lovely" and "worthy," as all men should acknowledge.[16]

And this capacity to love God produces its own divine mandate—to love God's creations, human beings. From the love of God to men, says Edwards, comes the reciprocal love of humans to God and of "love to the people of God, and to mankind."[17] God "carries on a design of love to his people" so that saintly "love to God" and "Christian love to men" will follow.[18] Justification means a longing, in fact, precisely to "initiate that divine love manifested in Christ" and Christ's "practice" in society, to "make returns of love for love and so to love God and Christ and imitate [Christ's] love to men." "Love to God and man," says Edwards, "is the sum of all holiness."[19]

"We love one another as [God] hath loved us. [W]e *ought* to love one another as God hath loved us and as Christ hath loved us, and so [as a result] we shall be as he was," or at any rate shall strive to be as he was.[20] God alone, strictly speaking, has "beauty within himself" and "love of himself." The "excellence of others" must therefore be in "loving *others*." Everything "resolves into love," that inclination in the hearts of humans to love both God and other humans that is the most meaningful sign of rebirth.[21]

Love for Edwards was intrinsically social in its theological and doctrinal dimensions, involving adoration and affection within the Trinity, between God and humanity, and among humans and humans. And it was love in this social sense that would inform and suffuse the work of holiness, i.e., charity and community, that he hoped to see around him.

Genuine charity, the substance rather than the mere form of doing good, requires "love to God and men," a "love of benevolence" and "amiableness," "having love to one another."[22] Charity is "loving our neighbors" enough to give to them what is ours, thereby loving them in the way Christ loved us. It is "the sum of the moral law," a giving out of love to those made in God's image and of the same blood and thus following the rule to love "our neighbors as ourselves." Through the exercise of charity we show a "dear affection and concern" for the welfare of fellow Christians, "whom we should love as brethren" in the same way that Christ loved us.[23] "Love works no ill but all good . . . to our neighbor," Edwards never tires of repeating, since love to God and a "Christian love to men" are but one.[24] The balm of charity is how the "good of human society" is maintained, and how "love to God and love to men" are expressed. Therefore "express your love" and "abound in deeds of love and charity."[25]

Community, too, subsists in and requires love. This is partly a matter of human nature, of the inclinations of the natural unregenerate. "'Tis one of the simple laws of our nature, that we delight in being loved and valued by others," says Edwards, and also in loving others, which is a step toward togetherness since "that which men love, they desire to have and to be united to, and possessed of."[26] But it is also a matter of Christian faith, of love to God and obedience to Christ's command, that we love one another. Love to God and love to the saints, the "brethren," go together, so that "one never is without the other."[27] Love makes us "like-minded," united as members of the visible church, joined (in Paul's phrase) in a "bond of perfectness," with an "intimate affection" toward "fellow members" of Christ, a "fervent" love to them in the bowels of Jesus Christ, a "oneness of heart and soul."[28]

Every member of Christian society has "reigning in his heart a principle of peace and love." Love is the "bond of perfectness"—in eighteenth-century terms, a kind of moral gravity holding men to collective endeavor who would otherwise fly apart. Nor does it apply to saints alone: " 'Tis men's duty to love *all* whom they are bound . . . to look upon as the children of God," and to be, like God, "kind to the evil and the good."[29] Love is therefore all-encompassing. It is a "true love" of "all creatures," a meditation on "tranquility and peace," a "general love and delight, everywhere diffused." It is a love of "everything," the summum bonum of holiness.[30]

Edwards struggled, as did most ministers, to convey the feeling of divine and divinely inspired love, and he reached in doing so for analogies from ordinary life. One of the most powerful of these, or at least one that he used frequently, was romantic love, if we may use that term—the love of a man and a woman, or a man for a woman, like that he experienced as a youth at roughly the same time he was experiencing an overpowering sense of love to God. One may speculate that love worked itself so deeply into his work, and allowed him to discourse so freely about it throughout his life not only because of his Christian faith but because these two loves, to God and woman, enveloped him simultaneously at a crucial stage of his emotional and intellectual development. When Edwards discusses divine love, it is frequently in the terminology of a "lover" to his "beloved," of love as a "passion."

These are not precisely the same. The love of God, "as it is in the divine nature," is not exactly a passion, "is not such a love as we [ourselves] feel." But there are similarities. The highest evidence of love is not affectionate verbal expression, though that assuredly counts, but the "expense" or cost, i.e., the actual "sacrifice," that the act of love entails for the "lover"—as when God gave his son to us in the greatest of any conceivable "expense," the symbol of the love between God, Christ, and the church. God, through this holy incarnation, "is really become passionate to his own" and therefore loves with the kind of love "as we have to him or to those we most dearly love."[31]

Edwards is careful to give spiritual and divine love pride of place, but he does so within a frame of reference of passionate earthly love. "Earthly lovers" revel in the enjoyment of a shared sense of beauty, ardor, and intimacy. They will, however, eventually reach the end of their "discoveries of each other's beauty" and the limit of their "intimate" communion and will exhaust their "most endearing expressions." How happy, by contrast, is the prospect of divine and spiritual love, in which there is "eternal progress in all these things; [and] new beauties are continually discovered, and more and more loveliness," so that "we shall forever increase in beauty ourselves [and] our union will become more close, and communion more intimate"—spiritual love thus becoming a lyrical, near-mystical version of the familiar "joys" of earthly romance.[32] There is a difference, Edwards carefully insists, between "lust and love," which are "opposite principles." Love is more than passion. Passion, as he observed during the Great Awakening, is more violent and sudden, leaving the mind overpowered and the emotions uncontrolled. Love is bliss.[33]

There is a romantic element in Edwards's discussion of the dove as a symbol of God's "infinite love and delight." The dove is a bird "beyond all other irrational animals" in its "remarkable and wonderful" love to its mate, which it expresses by "billing . . . and the like while together," and in "mourning for the loss" of its mate at death. A dove, he continues, was "appointed to be offered in sacrifice" in early times precisely because it symbolized "love."[34] Edwards wrote these particular lines in or about the winter of 1725–1726, before assuming the mantle of Solomon Stoddard's Northampton ministry and when he was still, we may suppose, in the throes of his adoration of Sarah Pierpont, but similar comparisons and imagery appear throughout his work. Two years later he calls "the relation between Christ and the church" like a man's with his wife, a "virtuous and pious and pure love between a man and his spouse," very much an "amorous disposition" of the "Spirit of God."[35] Still later the dove recurs as an emblem, along with the ceremonial olive branch and oil of anointment, of love and peace.[36]

Edwards notes the way a man will offer himself, and "joint possession of his estate," to a woman if she will "receive him and unite herself" to him. "Here," he says, is Christ's offering himself to sinners if they accept him by faith and "open the door to let him in."[37] Christ loves individual persons the same way individual lovers love only one other person. "The man Christ Jesus loves believers, not only the church in general" but the believer "in particular." But he loves the church en masse as well because it is "made up of those particular persons that he loves." He loves, like an earthly lover, all "loveliness."[38] Christ thus focuses on the saints individually and collectively, "delighting to have his spouse," the church, "show her love to him" as the "pleasant fruits" that she "lays up for her beloved."[39] A wife merely caring conscientiously for her husband without genuine "love" is "wooden," as is a man showing devotion to God without a heart filled with love.[40] A Christian should be a "true" lover.[41]

Edwards paired love, as he paired light and other conceits, with familiar emotional words—with joy, happiness, delight, sweetness, beauty, kindness, relish.[42] God's love is "favor" and "delight," Christ's love is "reverential" and "inexpressibly sweet."[43] Love could be intellectual and also aesthetic. The "primary and original beauty or excellence that is among minds," writes the young Edwards, is in fact "love."[44] Feelings about beautiful buildings or music are at bottom "love."[45] Love, he says at age fifty as he struggles still to convey its sense, may not be unlike admiration for persons of fine character or of similar education or taste or of pronounced benevolence.[46]

He commonly associates gospel love with family feelings, praising the loving spirit and "disposition and temper" of a "dutiful child," and urging that we should appear in "sweet childlike love" before God, to whom we stand as children. We should feel a duty to love "kindred" spirits, those "near and dear" to us, as "children of God," for the "spirit of a child . . . is love" and foreshadows our union to God as his children.[47] He tells parents to make sure, "if you love your children," that they are beyond the reach of Satan, are safe in Christ, whose relation to God is after all filial.[48] He encapsulates the point in a sermon during the Great Awakening: "Children Ought to Love the Lord Jesus Christ Above All."[49]

As to other family feeling, he calls Christ "our kinsman and brother," whose life was a "work of love to us."[50] Members of the church are "brethren," of "one family" in a "common society that Christian brethren have together."[51] Edwards praises (glossing the language of the gospels and Paul) "brotherly love," "love of the brethren," "cleaving" to one another with "brotherly natural strong endearments," showing "unfeigned love" of brethren.[52] Christians must "love as brethren . . . as Christ has loved us."[53] Love is "that common society that Christian brethren have together." The Sermon on the Mount contains moral precepts respecting "neighbors and brethren."[54] "He that loves not his brethren," writes the aging Edwards, drawing upon child imagery in a paraphrase of I John, "is a child of the devil."[55]

Beyond family are friends. A saint's love to God, though more rewarding, resembles a man's love for a friend whom he desires to please and honor, so that he dreads death from fear of losing this friendship.[56] Loving God, our "Father and friend," sweetens the comforts of the godly.[57] Loving Christ brings the "sweetest delights of love and friendship."[58] A Christian, Edwards says, invoking friends and friendship at times almost as a drumbeat or litany, must be a "real and hearty friend," and as with friends, so with neighbors because love to neighbors, he constantly repeats, "is the sum of the moral law."[59] Religion is "loving God with all our hearts, with all our souls, and with all our minds, and our neighbor as ourselves."[60]

Visible members of the church, God's saints, especially share the gift of love, which at its heights is "exceeding great and vigorous; impressing the heart with the strongest and most lively sensation of inexpressible sweetness, mightily moving, animating, and engaging them, making them like to a flame of fire." True saints are "loving, benevolent and beneficent."[61] Love is the "bond that unites" the visible saints and makes them "likeminded" and "amiable" and one in "body and soul."[62] Saints, Edwards says, conflating family metaphors, are "the children of Abraham," the "seed of Jesus Christ," and the "offspring of God," are "of one family" and, if truly full of grace, love "as brethren."[63]

Conveying the nature of divine and human love was not easy, and at one point when Edwards was past forty, after more than two decades of trying, he all but capitulated: "As to a definition of divine love, things of this nature are not properly capable of a definition. They are better felt than defined."[64] Yet he was soon back at it, arguing, as he had as a youth, that love's relation to religion is clear, and that the "sum of all religion," of all "true religion," consists in "great part" of this "holy affection" of love. Religion is a "vigorous fervent love," is "summarily comprehended in love," is the totality of what was "taught and prescribed in the law and the prophets" and by Christ.[65] Before his death he makes one last effort. The result is formal but simple, as clear and encompassing in its way as he or anyone ever managed: Love is a being's "being dear to us" and our desiring "welfare" for him or her and therefore "union."[66]

It goes without saying, although Edwards said it often enough, that men must love "all" members of the community with a "liberal, bountiful grace."[67] Loving "all," however, raised thorny issues because Edwards, like all ministers, daily faced the depressing evidence of the narrowness of people's love and their inability to do what Scripture explicitly directs: to love others. This was a preoccupation of religious ethicists as well as ministers and a favorite topic of eighteenth-century thinkers, and it posed theoretical and practical challenges for Edwards in two particular areas. One was how to extend the boundaries of love beyond the self, the other how to extend those boundaries beyond the pale—to one's enemies.

Edwards believed that a narrow self-love is antithetical to loving God and behaving for the common good, a point broached early, repeated frequently, and fully elaborated in *History of Redemption* (preached in 1739, published in 1774) and *True Virtue* (published 1765) and in his notes for the latter. He argues that "confined self-love" and "confined selfishness" are the opposite of "general benevolence."[68] Self-love of this kind—"selfishness"—engenders "self-vindication," an "aggrandizing" self that will lead to anger and the "desire of revenge." This is the antithesis of "true virtue," which consists of "love . . . or benevolence to being in general," or the enlarging of oneself to "take [others] in."[69] Confined self-love engenders "self-conceit," a proud, "hypocritical," deceiving, even self-deceiving affectation that makes love to others both partial and temporary.[70] Self-love becomes in this way a "private affection" reflecting an "abhorrent," "base," "sordid" spirit. It fuses a person to himself alone or, just as bad, to another "particular person or private system," a single favored person or favored group, rather than to "all." The Fall, intones Edwards, so twisted man's soul that he lost his "nobler and more extensive principles" and fell under the "government of self-love."[71]

Constricted self-love is singularly deceptive and treacherous, according to Edwards, because the "natural" unregenerate who lack true love may exhibit virtuous traits—love to friends, a desire to please, admiration for honor or strength or learning, an appreciation of justice and wise policy. But this is far from the enduring and encompassing Christian love of charity, men, Christ, Scripture, and God. Indeed, left to themselves without faith, natural men show signs of "distemper, melancholy, doctrinal ignorance, prejudices of education" and "peculiar temptations," and they therefore falter in holiness, humility, and the universality of their love, which becomes temporary, evanescent, shrunken, limited.[72]

But self-love of a narrow kind can also make it difficult to act upon what for Edwards was a cardinal principle of the gospel—loving one's enemies. We have a "gospel" duty, a "new" duty, of "heartily loving enemies." Men pretend not to hate their enemies, "but they really do." Yet Christians should "love their enemies from their hearts," do good to "them that do evil to them," and forgive "those that injure them." Christ teaches that "our enemies, those that abuse and injure us, are our neighbors" and must be loved as "ourselves."[73] Edwards did not argue that this should be true in all circumstances. He was pacific, but not a pacifist. King David, living under the Mosaic injunction to love one's neighbors, in fact prayed against his enemies, Edwards notes, but only because they threatened God's kingdom, Israel. We must love and protect our own public and people of God in the same way—by, for example, warding off the French and their Indian allies. But David, though a pre-Gospel man, did not pray against his enemies as individuals, and neither should we.[74] A Christian's ultimate weapons, we should always remember, are not in any case carnal but spiritual. They must be wielded from love, not hate. Whatever protective measures might be entailed, Christians must in the end "love their enemies," whether distant heathens or papists or (Edwards notes acerbically) those dwelling more closely who spitefully use us.[75]

This duty, he argues, is especially pronounced from the time of the Gospels. Mosaic law provided us with the means to transcend the self—to love our neighbors. Gospel law more explicitly expands the meaning of "neighbors" to "all." Since "gospel times," says Edwards, it has been "requisite that all ceremonial commands should be abolished" that have neither intrinsic "agreeableness to the lovely God" nor (which demonstrates this Gospel faith's social dimension) any "tendency to happiness."[76] The new commandment to love demands more because it "requires that we love one another as Christ hath loved us." And this must encompass enemies.[77]

Edwards made much of this shift from Judaism to Christianity, which is therefore in his view at bottom a spiritual rather than a legalistic faith. He understood that law, man's as well as God's, was essential to human society at all times. But "if ye are led by the Spirit," Edwards argues, "you don't need the law, for the Spirit produces the fruits that the law obliges to, without being under the exaction of the law"—that is, without coercion, without constable or jailor or prison. At some level there is hardly a need for the law: "The spirit of love fulfills the law." Love is "the fulfilling of the law," the very "principle of a Christian's obedience," the "sum of Christian holiness."[78]

Love is both adjunct and alternative to formal laws, which, though appropriate and necessary to insure natural men's charitable and communal behavior, are inferior to saintly love, which acts freely, therefore genuinely, from humble obedience to God and in imitation of Christ, thus precluding the need for coercion and punishment.[79] "Slavish fear," says Edwards, is a "servile principle," the spirit of mere "bondage." The Spirit of God casts out fear with the "prevailing of love." Love "drives away all fear."[80] Edwards understood man-made law to be necessary, having worked for a poor relief fund and argued for the preservation of the Massachusetts Bay charter that guarantees the privileges of the Congregational churches. But he also clearly sensed the risk of untrammeled force in human affairs, whether in the form of the absolutist tyranny of papist France or the heavy-handedness and corruption of the British authorities. Love in this sense is a palliative of power and an alternative to the coercion of the law.

Edwards also meant by "fear" the fear of God's eternal punishment, the last judgment and consignment of the unregenerate to hell, a fear that he exploited, like many others, in sermons such as "Sinners" and in imprecatory preaching during the revivals.[81] Yet love is always the ultimate goal. "Fear of hell" is a "slavish, tormenting principle; but as love prevails it delivers people from this tormenting, grievous principle."[82] God, to be sure, does not "wholly cast out fear, the legal principle," and ministers may call up fear as warranted. "When love is low in the true saints," Edwards explains to a Scottish correspondent, "they need the fear of hell to deter them from sin . . . but when love is high, and the soul full of it, we don't need fear."[83] The "obedience of natural man and a gracious obedience differ." The one is merely forced. "The other obeys from love with delight" and exercises, "from choice and with cheerfulness," the "free, universal and disinterested love and beneficence" and "noble disposition" of the Christian.[84]

Edwards never forgot in all his observations about human love and its place in society that love to God should precede love to men in the same way that it should accompany the influx of grace. He writes in the 1720s that the "new duties" of the gospel rest on revelations concerning the Trinity and the love of God and Christ, which will lead in turn to "the denying of ourselves"—the transcendence of one's own self—and the "loving of our enemies with a sincere love"—the transcendence of one's own group. Thence would come a "universal love to all mankind" and "loving one another as Christ has loved us."[85] He writes in the 1730s that "a life of love is sweet, but love to God is sweeter still, a "purer flame"; in the 1740s, that the "fear and love of God" leads to love to men, saints, and enemies and a spirit of service to God and mankind; in the 1750s, that the "chief and most fundamental of all the commands of the moral law" requires us 'to love the Lord our God."[86] It is divine love that has the power to convert self-love into love or affection for "all."[87] The pathway to love to others and the forming of a holy charitable community is regeneration—the transformation of the heart through submission to the love and power of God and the flowering of a "complex" or "public" love.[88]

Edwards despaired at times of achieving his lofty goals. As he writes in a letter in 1739, "I don't know what more I can say." One explanation for this momentary despair is that the Connecticut Valley Revival had faltered, and community behavior, as in the meeting house controversy, was profoundly disappointing. Another explanation might be that he had worked himself into a closed box of perfectionism. This is in part simply the normal consequence of living the life of a minister devoted to transforming wayward congregations. It was also in part the burden of what George Marsden calls a "perfectionist" personality that insisted on an impossible ideal of holiness, one that required people to sell everything, submerge their egos, treat others as themselves, love their enemies—"too high hopes," as Marsden puts it, for a sinful world.[89]

But Edwards did not give up. He participated in the Great Awakening, supported the international prayer movement, crafted a doctrine of "true virtue"—all efforts, in a sense, to break out of the perfectionist box he had constructed for himself. He also combed Scripture for plausible models of societies devoted to God and blessed with God's love. And he found three: Israel in the time of Solomon, the age of the Millennium as prophesied in Scripture, and Heaven itself.

Israel in the reign of Solomon was a "most glorious time," writes Edwards in his biblical notes, when the Israelites were the "greatest empire in the world," and every "heathen nation" from the Euphrates to Egypt took notice. King Solomon, who enjoyed the Lord's promise of support, used it to enlarge the national frontiers and spread his fame to the "utmost bounds" of the world so that the heathen would see "the God of Israel" and have "knowledge of him." He built a temple of magnificent "strength and beauty" and a chariot of wood from Lebanon with silver pillars, a gold bottom, and purple covering, "the midst thereof being paved with love." He possessed hundreds of wives and concubines (forbidden by the Law but tolerated, Edwards speculates somewhat ruefully, as emblems of Solomon's stature as God's ruler) and hundreds of horses, and he took Pharaoh's daughter as his spouse. There was wealth from industry and trade, so that God's people were able to take their rest in this pacified and prosperous "church state of the Jews." There was music and love poetry and the devotional songs of the Canticles and Psalms, and the times were "glorious," "happy," and "holy."[90]

But while the Hebrews were God's chosen people, they were, unhappily, pre-Christian and therefore not wholly adequate as a model, particularly since in the end Solomon led them away from proper sacrifice and worship and thus doomed them to captivity. So Edwards, in addition to acknowledging the prosperity and holiness of Solomon's reign, interpreted the era typologically. The dazzling materials of Solomon's chariot symbolize the brightness and dignity of Christ (silver), his suffering (purple), his "everlasting covenant" (cedar), his eternal "electing" love (the chariot bottom).[91] The love songs of Canticles do not refer to a "particular woman" but to "a society, even that holy society, the church of God." Canticles devoted to a "spouse" were not epithalamia for an actual female bride but mystical hymns celebrating the future espousal of Christ with his church. The songs describing the beloved's breasts as two twin roes feeding among the lilies represent the "chastity and purity" and means of grace of the church of Christ, as do the many references to pairs—of golden pipes, of olive trees, of testaments and sacraments and (from Revelation) witnesses. "The two breasts" mean love, but "love to God and love to men" rather than romance. The song is divine because "the bridegroom is Christ."[92]

The crowning of Solomon at his marriage to the daughter of Pharaoh is at one level the church's crowning of Christ when church and Christ marry. At another level it represents, Edwards argues, the "last and most glorious times of the church," the "great gathering of the Gentiles," an event that points, by way of typology, to another model of holy society—the Millennium that is prophesied in the book of Revelation and other scriptural passages.[93]

The Millennium, the long age preceding the Second Coming that Edwards addressed at some length in his early notebooks and sermons and in *An Humble Attempt* and the sermon series *History of the Work of Redemption,* was, in his mind, a logical higher stage of attainment and a rich source of suggestions as to the nature of holy Christian society. Millennialism enjoyed a rich history among Christians, much of it so extravagant and violence-prone that Church authorities sought to suppress it. Milder forms of millennial preaching, common in early New England, were becoming somewhat rarer by the time of Edwards, whose depictions, though unlike the chiliastic effusions of earlier centuries, could be fulsome.[94]

Edwards argues that during the coming Millennium, which might last a thousand years or much longer, the work of Christ will prevail across the globe and make the world "more like Heaven." One part of this will be material, the result of "contrivances and inventions" such as the mariner's compass that will provide "easy and safe communication" between distant regions and hasten the "tedious voyage" from hemisphere to hemisphere and thus open "the countries about the poles" to us. Already, Edwards notes, global communication has increased through the "flourishing of arts and sciences," navigation in particular, and this will dramatically increase in "the glorious times" leading to the actual Millennium, at which time "all useful arts shall be carried to the highest perfection."[95] Men will be able to conduct their "necessary secular business" more easily and productively, enabling them to produce more but also to have time for "more noble exercises."[96] Business will be conducted not for private gain or accumulating wealth for posterity but for necessities and "for Christ" and a glorious church.[97] The result will be "great temporal prosperity."[98] Wealth will abound, there will be no war, life will be longer, and families and populations will grow, multiplying a million-fold by the end of this age.

Knowledge will increase and spread, a marvelous boon in the view of learned New Englanders such as Edwards. There will be "many excellent books" and "wonderful performances" and a zeal for instruction.[99] Neither religious nor secular learning will be "imprisoned within only two or three nations of Europe," but expand across the world, "the various parts of it mutually enlightening each other." Barbarous nations will become "as bright and polite as England," and ignorant heathen lands will enjoy "profound divines and most learned philosophers." There will be "wondrous discoveries, admirable books of devotion, the most divine and angelic strains" from Hottentots and Terra Australis alike, who will enjoy the advantage of the sentiments of learned men of the most distant nations. The "press shall groan" in wild Tartary. "What infinite advantages will they have for discovering the truth of every kind!"[100]

There will be, more importantly, universal Christian faith, with the "whole earth . . . united as one holy city, one Heavenly family." Men of "all nations" will dwell together and "will be one and act as one, all members living as brothers" and experiencing "extraordinary joy" to "all being on earth and in Heaven." The Jews will "look upon all the world to be their brethren," and become once more God's people as of old, but conjoined now with Gentiles, "Mohammedans," heathens, deists, and Arminians. There will be no factions or false teaching in the churches, which will harbor worship, not superstition (a slap against Roman Catholics). Religion will "prevail" in a single "amiable society," and "peace, love and harmony will rule among saints." Religion will be "inscribed on every thing, on all men's common business and employments" and the "common utensils of life."[101] Religion will take possession of "palaces and thrones," princes and paupers will exchange places, and the rich will devote "all to Christ and his church."[102] There will be "excellent order" in "church discipline and government" and much beauty of the kind Edwards relished, and he waxes lyrical at the prospect of the world become "one church, one orderly, regular, beautiful society, one body, all the members in beautiful proportion." This church will be "beautiful and glorious," a "perfection of beauty," the "greatest image of Heaven."[103]

Love will pervade the Millennium, says Edwards, drawing liberally on Isaiah as well as Revelation. There will be "great peace and love" among nations instead of confusion and bloodshed. There will also be peace and love between "one man and another" and between "rulers and ruled" and "ministers and people." In place of "malice and envy and wrath and revenge" will flourish meekness, forgiveness, gentleness, and kindness—the "Christian virtues" of the "lovely" Jesus.[104] Despotic kings will give way in civil affairs to kings acting as judges similar to those of old Israel or the monarchs of present-day England. The result will liberate men "from the tyrannical and absolute power of men." There will be "true liberty" and a state in which all love God, one another, and their rulers, who will return their love.[105]

Although now, the mid-eighteenth century, is a "dark time" for religion, says Edwards, the prophecy of the Millennium should keep our hopes kindled. It will come not suddenly but soon enough, and by preaching and "ordinary means of grace," not through war or princely authority or miracles—through awakenings well-honed, with "instruments . . . improved and succeeded," and missions and missionaries such as David Brainerd enlightening "one nation . . . after another" and "one flock after another" like the mustard seed that ultimately fructifies.[106] The Millennium will far surpass the age of Solomon in its glory, and will comprise countless millions of souls where there are now mere thousands.[107] There will be "great rejoicing."[108] It will be a time of love, peace, knowledge, prosperity, charity, grace, and virtue, the realization of a vision of a world of goodness that men like Edwards and missionaries like Brainerd should strive toward by taking every advantage of the current great advances in learning and communication.

Yet however compelling and hopeful, the Millennium will be only a way station, a harbinger the way Solomon's Israel was a harbinger. It will not be the true "end times." Though long-lasting, it will culminate in a humanity grown "insensible to sin" and a final Great Apostasy in which the forces of Antichrist and Satan will avail themselves, as the saints had, of modern means of communication to achieve dominion.[109] Only then will Christ come again, scattering the forces of darkness, consigning the sinful to hell, and raising the souls of the saints to the bosom of God in Heaven.

Thus the Millennium, though glorious, will be merely transitional because it will be ephemeral and bound to end. It will also be, despite its marvelous qualities, only an extension, in a sense, of familiar earthly existence—ample material prosperity, but still material, derived largely from technology and trade; spiritual and material advances, but based still on projections from the past (Solomon's realm) and the present (the compass and telescope, books, eighteenth-century preaching). Love and peace will reign, but egos will remain. There will be universal grace and love of God, but not union with him. There will be imitation of Christ, but not oneness with him.

It will not be, in a word, Heaven. Edwards, a staunch millennialist, always understood the ultimate goal of the saints to be the "light, sweetness, and blessedness of Heaven, that world of love" that transcends prophecy and knowledge and gives rise to "eternal life."[110] The church is "progressive before the resurrection . . . with a progression of preparation for another more perfect state" where we will be "eternally happy!"[111] Revelation shows us the "new Jerusalem," the church in her "happy state." This refers to the Christian church "on earth" following the destruction of "Antichrist and the other public enemies of the church," and also to the "triumphant state of the church in Heaven." Some parts of this particular Scriptural passage, writes Edwards, clearly concern the Millennium—"nations walking in light," kings bringing honor and glory, plants whose leaves heal. But much of it signifies the "triumphant, sinless, and immortal state" following the resurrection.[112] The Millennium will be "more like heaven" in "contemplative and spiritual" ways, God's way of "gradually" bringing the "design of his mercy to their consummation as an architect gradually erects and completes a building." But it will not be in fact Heaven.[113] The Millennium is the more or less describable possibility of earthly joy. Heaven is the near-indescribable prospect of ultimate joy.[114]

What are the features of the Edwardsian Heaven? Different and wondrous, he says, so that "if we search all the face of earth, and . . . tear out its bowels and ransack its innards, or dive to the bottom of the sea, go and look into the palaces and stately rooms of princes, and search their coffers" and "take in the visible Heavens" and imagine them "better and more beautiful than they are, we can get nothing that will serve to give us a picture of Heavenly glory."[115] And most significantly, Heaven will be fundamentally social—an ideal template for judging the kind of holy community Edwards longed to approximate.

The particular details of the world of Heaven are less important than the overall conception, but they are nonetheless of interest and significance.[116] There will be abundance, certainly, but of an Edenic kind—fruits in plenty and of many varieties that flourish anew without human toil, and crystal-clear water from an eternally flowing spring—meaning a surcease of the heavy labor that eighteenth-century people, especially in rural New England, knew so terribly well. This is a more or less predictable vision given the received Christian wisdom about Eden and the way Edwards viewed the peaceful abundance of Solomon's Israel and the Millennium.

There will be "many mansions" and many rooms. There will be streets of pure but "transparent" gold that show none of the grubbiness of earthly cities where streets are defiled by dirty feet that need constant washing.[117] There will be no charity because there will be no poverty, and no "rulers" in human form even in the guise of judges. There will be much singing because singing is beautiful.[118] Christ will have a throne surrounded by multitudes of saints and angels holding "intimate conversation" and "sharing ideas" with one another, yet remaining all the while in perfect harmony with the "supreme Mind" of God, to whose "inexhaustible fountain" of love they will "open their bosoms."[119] The Heavenly world will be on the one hand "progressive," in the sense of constantly moving and shifting toward ever more loveliness, and on the other hand eternal and infinite—enduring "forever and ever" within an "endless expanse."[120]

There will be light, the intense "resplendent" light of the "glorified bodies" and "countenances" of the saints and "the man Jesus Christ" and of God "if there shall be any visible appearance representing the presence of the Deity." Christ's face will have a more "excellent and delightful sort of refulgence" than the light of this world, as will the faces of the saints. Heaven will be "pleasant to us," says Edwards, because (deploying favored tropes) the light is "sweet" and "harmonious" and the sensation of it "pleasant to the mind" and "easy and pleasant to behold!"[121] Heavenly light will pass through an unimaginably fine medium, he speculates, revealing, as it bounces from the dazzling figures of Christ and the saints, a "ravishing proportion of reflections" and "beauties and harmonies altogether of another kind from what we perceive here." What's more, we will perceive all this mentally, with our minds—with "immediate intellectual views of minds . . . more immediate, clear and sensible" than with "bodily eyes."[122]

Sound, too, will travel "infinitely farther with exactness" rather than moving sluggishly (says this student of Newton) through "particles." And our ability to hear will be "exquisitely perceptive." In Heaven the saints will be able to "distinguish in the greatest multitude of sounds" their distance and direction by ear "more exactly than we do by the eye." We cannot even conceive, in fact, "how far they may clearly hear one another's discourses."[123] "For aught we know," says Edwards, they may see one another's beauty and hold "delightful" and "intimate conversation, at a thousand miles' distance."[124] And God may contrive other "inconceivable" configurations of "quite a different kind"—"exquisite spiritual proportions" between "one spiritual act and another, between one disposition and another, and between one mind and another, and between all their minds and Christ Jesus and the supreme mind, and particularly between the man Christ Jesus and the Deity, and among the persons of the Trinity, the supreme harmony of all."[125]

This heightened ability to see and hear and connect is crucial because of the thoroughly social nature of Edwards's Heaven. It contains "many millions" of souls, all the saints from all of human history, who have various types of interconnections and relationships, so that the ability to see or hear vast numbers over immense distances is crucial.[126] Edwards sometimes describes this in family terms, with Christ as the father, the prophets and apostles and saints that were in life "great lights" as wives and mothers, and other saints as older or younger children.[127] Christ elsewhere stands as the saints' "representative, their brother, and the husband of the church" and his divine Father's obedient Son.[128] And besides family there is friendship—for why would they not enjoy those affections in Heaven who loved one another with a "virtuous love" and showed a loving kindness in life? This "special respect for another" is pleasing to

God, who created us as "special instruments" of friendship and neighborliness.[129]

"The heaven I desired," recalled Edwards of his youth, "was a heaven
of holiness; to be with God, and to spend my eternity in divine love.
. . . My mind was very much taken up with contemplations on heaven.
. . . There the saints could express their love." Edwards's Heaven is God-
centric because God, at the pinnacle of the Heavenly social pyramid, is
"the lawgiver and absolute sovereign" who rules wisely and justly, and the
saints rejoice to serve him, confident that he knows what is best for "his
glory and the good of the blessed society."[130]

But God is also the chief focus of saintly love, a fact that has its own
implications. It makes, for example, the saints' "subjection" to God's
rule simply the exercise of "unfeigned and perfect" love to him—true
love as an "active principle."[131] It also subsumes other relationships, those
"shadow affections" of fathers and mothers, husbands, wives, or children,
or the "company of earthly friends" that offer clues to Heavenly community, but are nevertheless mere "scattered beams" while "God is the
sun"—mere "streams, but God is the ocean."[132]

Such concentrated and overwhelming love to God makes Heaven a
world of tranquility because it soothes the saints' previously troubled
hearts. On earth, men sometimes know a degree of comfort but also
unease; sweetness but also sorrow; light but also dark. Not so in Heaven.
There, for the first time since the Fall from Eden, they will be united
with God, whose presence will "possess" their hearts and be an antidote
to grief and pain. Enmity will become love. Pride and envy will melt into
community. Obedience to authority will be not only bearable but wonderful. The terrible disquiet of the human heart will be gone.[133]

Edwards took pains to make clear that Heaven is a place of social ranks
and gradations, but these will have a far different significance than here
on earth, where they are essential but troubling. While Edwards occasion-
ally assumes that a system of specialized individual graces will blend—
"concatenate"—into a unified Heavenly whole, thus accommodating a
lingering whiff of individual personality, more typically he sees a well-
ordered constellation of spiritual ranks—God at its pinnacle, prophets
and apostles next highest, ministers and the deeply holy just below that,
then saints of varying degrees of grace and so on, with the saints in turn

closer to God than the angels. Some may be exalted in glory above others, and some happier than others, but no matter. These are spiritual, not material, ranks with no correspondence to earthly riches and power. It will therefore "not damp any" to see others loved more than themselves: "They shall have as much love as they desire and as great manifestations of love as they can bear." And they themselves will love those above or below them on the spiritual ladder. "Such will be the union of all of them, that they will be partakers of each other's glory and happiness."[134]

There will be no self-righteousness, hence neither pride nor envy. On the contrary, all are "holy and shining with the beauty of Jesus," happy for all others, in whose countenances they after all see the image of God.[135] Paul Ramsey is therefore correct: The common denominator of this Edwardsian vision of Heaven is "the primacy of society."[136]

Edwards, like Dante, had difficulty with the details of Heaven since these derived, for both men, ultimately from vague biblical prophecy, personal imagination, and a sense of what might constitute absolute holiness. Hell was a good deal more vivid for both, although for neither did it always involve fire. Edwards argued that if Heaven is pure love, hell must be the opposite—a place where there is no love, a place deluged not only with fire but with wrath and hatred and rage, a place of pride and contention and strife and of spite, treachery, fickleness, hypocrisy, and deceit. It is a place without friendship or pity or mercy. This is as compelling a definition of hell as any minister ever offered. Though there is plenty of room for fire, in the end hell is the place without love.[137]

This makes "Heaven Is a World of Love," the sermon that concludes *Charity and Its Fruits,* all the more poignant and powerful. This sermon is not well known compared to other works, possibly because it was not published until the mid-nineteenth century, more likely because it seems so poor a fit with Edwards's fierce reputation. Some biographers treat it in a few paragraphs, others not at all. Most of the numerous recent collections of essays on Edwards are similarly neglectful.

The sermon deserves better. Wilson Kimnach considers it fully equal to "Sinners in the Hands of an Angry God" in rhetorical power and brilliance; Paul Ramsey calls it essential to a full understanding of Edwards.[138] These are, if anything, understatements. Heaven, says Edwards here, is a world not just of love but of perfect love, and in this sermon he explains why. As he does so, he reaches as far into the human heart and its anxieties and longings as it is possible for a pulpit minister to reach. At a purely emotional level, the result is all but overwhelming. A summary will serve as an appropriate climax to this chapter.

In Heaven, Edwards says, we will be able to love God, Christ, and one another perfectly, without envy or malice or revenge or contempt or selfishness. In Heaven no one will ever be grieved that they are slighted by those they love. Nor will the joy of Heavenly love be interrupted by jealousy. "Heavenly lovers," in Edwards's words, "will have no doubt of the love of each other. All their expressions of love shall come from the bottom of their hearts." In Heaven there will be nothing to clog the exercise and expression of love—no heavy body or lump of flesh or unfit organ or inadequate tongue. We shall have no difficulty expressing our love. Our souls, "like a flame of fire with love, shall not be like a fire pent up but shall be perfectly at liberty, winged with love with no weight tied to the feet to hinder their flight." Nor will there be any wall of separation to prevent the perfect enjoyment of each other's love—neither physical distance, nor want of full acquaintance, nor misunderstanding, nor disunion through difference of temperament or circumstances or opinions or interests. We shall all be united, related to Christ, the head of the whole society, the spouse of the whole church of saints, which shall be a single family.[139]

As love seeks to have the beloved for its own, so in Heaven all shall have property in one another. The saints shall be God's, and he theirs. And so with Christ, who bought them with his life and gave himself to them in death. "And the saints shall be one another's," and they shall enjoy each other's love in perfect and undisturbed prosperity, without adversity or pitiful grief of spirit, and shall glory in the possession of all things in common. And Heaven will be a garden of pleasure, a paradise fitted in all respects for an abode of Heavenly lovers where they may have sweet society. "The very light which shines in and fills that world is the light of love," says Edwards. "It is beams of love; for it is the shining of the glory of the Lamb of God, that most wonderful influence of lamblike meekness and love which fill the Heavenly Jerusalem with light."[140]

And we will know such perfect love forever, with no fear that our happiness will ever end. "All things," Edwards says in one of his most poignant moments, "shall flourish in an eternal youth. Age will not diminish anyone's beauty or vigor, and there love shall flourish in everyone's breast, as a living spring perpetually springing, or as a flame which never fails. And the holy pleasure shall be as a river which ever runs, and is always clear and full. There shall be no autumn or winter; every plant shall be in perpetual bloom with the same undecaying pleasantness and fragrance, always springing forth, always blossoming, always bearing fruit."[141]

He concludes in language tailored to appeal to a hard-driving, hard-driven, contentious, exhausted, anxious rural populace struggling to flourish at the far edge of civilization: "O what tranquility there is in such a world as this! Who can express the sweetness of this peace? What a calm is this, what a Heaven of rest is here . . . after persons have gone through a world of storms and tempests, a world of pride, and selfishness, and envy, and malice, and scorn, and contempt, and contention, and war? What a Canaan of rest!"[142]

Gerald McDermott argues that Edwards's eschatology, his understanding of the Millennium and the life of Heaven, was a social critique, a vision that constituted an implicit criticism of the extant social order.[143] There is support for this interpretation in the soaring ecstatic language of the "Heaven" sermon, its palpable longing for peace, union, and communion, and its brief but startling references to collective ownership and complex marriage ("all shall have property in one another"). Though a perfectionist, Edwards was no true utopian. Though holding fast to the prospect of a coming millennial age, he did not believe that humanity could in fact achieve Heaven on earth. If Heaven is love and hell is hate, this world is a mixture. To find true and perfect love, one must enter Heaven, which will only come through grace.

Yet he ends this magnificent sermon by telling his congregation, and all Christians and all humanity, that they should do the best they can here on earth—that "as Heaven is a world of love, so the way to Heaven is the way of love. This will prepare you for Heaven, and make you ready for an inheritance with the saints in that land of light and love. And if ever you arrive at Heaven, faith and love must be the wings that carry you there."[144]

AFTERWORD

The Bible is on the side of the poor, the impecunious and the destitute. He whom the Bible calls God is on the side of the poor. Therefore the Christian attitude to poverty can consist only of a corresponding allegiance.

— KARL BARTH

The exclusion of the weak and insignificant, the seemingly useless people, from a Christian community may actually mean the exclusion of Christ; in the poor brother Christ is knocking at the door.

— DIETRICH BONHOEFFER

THE POSITIONING of Edwards as pre-eminently a minister of a gospel of love represents a significant modification of his age-old reputation as a hellfire revivalist, a pessimistic prophet of eternal damnation, and an insensitive critic of the weaknesses of the flesh. He could be all these on occasion, but those occasions were not only largely tactical, means to an end, but rarer than when he filled his sermons with the poetry of light, beauty, harmony and sweetness, and the ethics of true Christian faith. Neither was he simply a cloistered intellectual or rescuer of individual souls. He was, virtually from day one of his career, a profoundly social minister. He cared about individual souls. But he cared as well about creating a world of charity and community bound by love.

A minister cannot preach seriously about charity without prompting his parishioners to reflect, if only briefly, on the nature of their community, about who among them are poor and how many and how poor and for what reason and what the implications might be for those who are not poor. Preaching about charity compels even the most resistant listeners to think, for a moment, about how best to deal with impoverished neighbors. It thus leads them to consider whom to help and how much and in what ways; and to think, as Edwards would have it, about how to help people without shredding their dignity and how to bring them more closely into the community. It also makes them conscious, if a minister is doing his job as well as Edwards did his, of the importance of not feeling superior to those in need or of being proud that they are givers, not recipients—and conscious that they themselves might someday be needy.

Preaching about charity prompts difficult reflection about helping not only neighbors but strangers or even, as the gospel teaches, enemies. It forces consideration of the true boundaries of community. Preaching about charity induces reflection, in other words, about the magnitude of responsibility—its reach and depth and the balancing of personal and collective resources on the one hand and human need on the other. Demanding from the pulpit evidence of charity as the true sign of grace prompts hard uncomfortable reflection in the pews, precisely as Edwards wanted it to prompt, about the relation between the influx of the Spirit and the practice of generosity.

Edwards preached as well about community and the need to strive for collective holiness, which is a kind of preaching that involves, for any minister, thinking hard about the nature of holy community. For Edwards a holy community was a place of gracious Christian behavior, meaning behavior with an inclusive common purpose as opposed to an exclusive individual one, a place where the overweening, aggrandizing self is restrained in the interest of a visible "public" and "complex" virtue that is simultaneously reverential, welcoming, and supportive. Edwards thought constantly about how to foster true community. He believed it required God's presence and therefore concerted effort on the part of the minister to bring the Divine into human hearts—and therefore concerted effort to welcome the Spirit into a town or congregation or country in the aggregate rather than simply individually.

Hence the various now-familiar measures such as revivals, missions, and collaborative prayer—accompanied, to be sure, by the occasional dollop of brimstone fear, a residue of his father and grandfather, and the more-than-occasional closely reasoned lecture on Christian ethics. Should the Spirit descend, the consequences would be apparent in improved community behavior. Should it not, there remained not only the law but the various rules of behavior embodied in, for example, the famous written Covenant of 1742: fair economic dealings, support for church and charity, and if not love for others then at least due respect for them. Anyone could and should adhere to these. Otherwise they would stand exposed as duplicitous opportunists devoid of all pretense of grace—as stand they did in Northampton in Edwards's eyes in the end.

Edwards must be seen, in light of all this, as an "improver," a reformer at the earthly as well as the spiritual level, the two being indissolubly welded in his mind. He was, strange though it sounds in a Calvinist context, actually an "optimistic" improver, as witness his unstinting efforts on behalf of, for example, group singing, collective prayer, community covenants, salvation *en masse,* a charitable fund, and the close reasoning of the well-known treatises over which he labored to the end—and for that matter the denial of sacraments to those who manifestly did not deserve them because their behavior toward one another showed no sign of grace.

George Marsden, Edwards's great biographer, attempts to capture this remarkable improving spirit: "Although Edwards is not usually thought of as a progenitor of the American party of hope, one can easily see continuities between *An Humble Attempt* [the trans-Atlantic prayer initiative] and reforming millennial optimism as late as 'The Battle Hymn of the Republic' or even into the progressive era."[1] The pursuit of the Millennium was a mark, as Marsden argues, of Edwards's optimistic devotion to the cause of holy community. So, it must be said, was his depiction of the joys of Heaven, the most inspiring and demanding model imaginable for the building of Christian community here in earth.

Love is the critical, indispensable ingredient, the means to the holy ends of charity and community. Edwards was a demanding minister. All improvers and reformers, including ministers, are demanding because they seek to challenge and change human behavior and human relations, and the more ambitious the reformer the greater the demands. None demanded more than Edwards, whose objective was to move men from absorption with self to sacrifice of self—to, in Edwards's terms, "giving without stint" and "sacrificing all." To give and sacrifice in this way, against one's own inclinations, requires a motive of great force: the absolute love for God and for humanity that stems from grace.

Love therefore becomes the most important concept and most important word in Edwards's vocabulary. God is a God of love. God loves humanity and all creation, and expects and deserves love in return not only for himself but for the humanity that he made in his image. Divine love transmuted to earth becomes the great enabler, the power that resolves division and conflict and takes us beyond the selfishness of acquisitiveness and miserliness, envy and pride, tribalism and sectarianism, provincialism and nationality. Love is the way to unity, which is a social concept whether with reference to union with God or with fellow saints, townspeople, or all humanity. Love advancing in harmony with learning, technology, and trade is what filled Edwards with hope for the coming of the good society.

The same social goals inform Edwards's depiction of Jesus Christ as a model for collective behavior as well as the incarnation of the deity. God's willingness to see his son die in atonement was his greatest gift to suffering humanity. But Edwards was prone to focus on Christ's life as well as his death, on Jesus as one of the working poor—self-sacrificing and meek under assault, forgiving of his enemies, willingly identifying himself with the downtrodden and outcast, rejecting the supplications and pretension of the rich, eschewing honors and office. For Edwards the preacher of grace, Christ represented sacrificial atonement. For Edwards the social minister, Christ was a model for saintly behavior, the purest exemplar of the virtues of generosity, tolerance, humility, self-sacrifice, and respect, the familiar Edwardsian litany of holy community behavior.

Edwards was hopeful because he had confidence in the redemptive power of God's love, but also because he saw human history as the divinely driven story of steady change. In this narrative, human society is not static but in a constant state of evolution and growth. Society in the flow of time represents movement by stages, with one stage leading more or less intelligibly, because guided by God, to the next from ancient times on into the future. God shapes developments, to be sure, for his purposes and ends, but in the form of a quasi-Hegelian rhythm of achievement, setback, and greater achievement. This is most striking in the point-counterpoint of Millennium, end times, and ascent to Heaven, but it appears as well, believed Edwards, in virtually every epoch of the six-thousand-year history of man on earth. Heaven itself leaves room for ever-increasing unity.

Perry Miller argues that Edwards perceived a "cyclical" pattern in the past that constituted "a dynamic process of realization within temporal

existence." Miller calls this, with only slight exaggeration, "such a metaphysical excursion as his contemporaries could not begin to comprehend."[2] In Edwards's own words, God's historical design is "carried on
not only by what is common to all ages but by successive works wrought
in different ages, all parts of one whole or one great step in each age and
another in another."[3] How, given this, could he not work optimistically
and hopefully to improve and reform?

Edwards's emphasis on charity, community, and love was neither original
nor unique among the clergy. Charity was an important strain in Christian thought, including Puritan thought, and Cotton Mather, Edwards's
near contemporary, wrote much about it. But Edwards was exception-
ally caustic and persistent in his condemnation of the uncharitable rich,
and he linked charitable behavior to the influx of grace with great force,
warning that rich men who did not give of their wealth were in fact not
Christians. Among his chief doctrinal adversaries were the ministers of
well-to-do Boston parishes who were increasingly reluctant to criticize
members of their own congregations. Better to preach individual liberty
and free trade than demand sacrifice for the public or the afflicted. On
this point Edwards seldom yielded.

Edwards preached the duty of charity as a divine injunction and because in the faces of the poor, as he argued on the basis of Scripture, one
sees the face of Jesus Christ. To give to a poor man is therefore to give to
Christ directly and personally. This notion, though again a familiar strain
in Christianity, was pronounced with Edwards, who depicted Jesus, his
family, his disciples, and his apostles as uneducated laboring people, a
view that seems less consonant on the whole with thinkers of the late
eighteenth century than of the seventeenth or even the middle and late
nineteenth centuries.

It seems consonant, for example, with Theodore Parker preaching on
the plight of the "perishing classes" of mid-nineteenth-century Boston,
classes who are perishing "soul and body, contrary to God's will; and
perishing all the worse because they die slow, and corrupt by inches"
because the great merchants of the city fail in their Christian duty to provide housing and education and even seats in the pews of great churches.
"Think not," says Parker in the accents of Edwards on charity, "I love

to speak hard words, and so often; say not that I am setting the poor against the rich. It is no such thing. I am trying to set the strong in favour of the weak."[4] It seems consonant, too, with Walter Rauschenbusch on the plight of industrial workers in the late nineteenth century—on the "chronic wretchedness" in our country and the fact that, again in the accents of Edwards, "if money dominates, the ideal cannot dominate. If we serve mammon, we cannot serve the Christ."[5]

It may be difficult to imagine Edwards standing with a Transcendentalist such as Parker, who, though concerned with the condition of the impoverished, lacked more or less by definition the kind of Christian grace that Edwards thought essential to encompassing and enduring virtue. It may be almost as difficult to align Edwards with Rauschenbusch, a Trinitarian, to be sure, but also a sympathizer with egalitarian democracy and the reordering of the economy. There was no industrial crisis in rural New England, though there may have been a spiritual crisis and times were always punishing and difficult, and therefore no conception of, or need for, any form of socialized production. Yet Edwards, Parker, and Rauschenbusch sounded similar notes with regard to charity, the poor, and the rich: Selfishness in the face of need is a sin against God and humanity.[6]

Would Edwards, who preached direct giving to the poor as God's representatives, have been comfortable with the "empire of benevolence" of the antebellum period, which began to routinize Christian good works, including not only evangelizing but soup kitchens, free clothing, and alms? Perhaps. He was already in his day comfortable with redistributive provincial and local arrangements. He would also, one presumes, have applauded the role of Presbyterians and Yale graduates in antebellum reform and how the benevolence empire often fused charity and salvation in the familiar Edwardsian way by means of the equally Edwardsian deployment of revivals and missions. Having long preached against means-testing for charity, he would not have found the distribution of charity by rules and regulations, a hallmark of centralized systems, overly bothersome even if he continued to urge face-to-face giving. We must give, he preached, even to the undeserving and obnoxious.

Edwards was also, it is important to remember, a believer in the coming of the Millennium. The mid-nineteenth century might have unexpectedly suggested, to Edwards as to many others, the dawn of a world-wide pre-Millennial spiritual surge that was being manifestly advanced by technological progress and the labors of the benevolence men—who after all distributed tens of thousands of copies of Edwards's own biography of David Brainerd, perhaps a compelling reason in itself for him to have welcomed the antebellum institutionalization of Christian charity represented by the empire of benevolence.[7]

Antebellum benevolence had many strands. Some would have been thoroughly congenial to Edwards, among them temperance, Sunday schools, sabbatarianism, the distribution of tracts and testaments, missionary work, and the distribution of goods to the poor, including to prisoners and the disabled. Devoted to the cause of social harmony, he would probably have found the vulgar rancor of Jacksonian politics un-Christian, antithetical to holiness, and thoroughly repulsive, a posture that aligns him with such eighteenth-century anti-party theorists as David Hume and the young James Madison, although where Hume and Madison would thwart bitterness and strife mainly with "mixed" government and constitutional machinery, Edwards, though appreciating checks and balances, would thwart it mainly with grace and love. But this same devotion to peace would almost certainly have drawn Edwards toward Thoreau and Lincoln in assailing the Mexican War.

The mention of Mexico inevitably raises the question of slavery. Edwards said little about slavery except in a draft letter criticizing the slave trade, and he owned house slaves at different times, as did other members of his family. Edwards did not question the institution of slavery any more than he questioned the institution of wage or indentured labor, and he not only owned slaves but employed wage servants, likely treating them in similar ways. He did have qualms about the slave trade, thought serious charity, including fair treatment, should extend to the economically disadvantaged, and thought all people of whatever race or condition were eligible for God's grace and the sacraments of the church. He performed marriage ceremonies for slaves, admitted them into his congregation, and manumitted at least one and possibly more. This may be contrasted with the views of a leading Boston minister, Charles Chauncy, whose anxieties about revivalism stemmed in part from its appeal to women, Africans, and the young.[8]

Slavery was not an issue in political discourse anywhere in the early and mid-eighteenth century, and some scholars have noted, in partial defense, that few white North Americans thought much about slavery before Edwards's death in the 1750s and still fewer opposed it. They note that the Bible, Edwards's main ethical text, seemed to sanction slavery, and that many ministers, even in New England, owned slaves. They note, too, that Edwards, more than most of his peers, considered Africans eligible for a place in Heaven, and that many of his followers became critics of both slavery and discrimination. Edwards himself had a strong faith-based understanding of justice and just desserts and the importance of charity, and these would almost certainly have drawn him more or less ineluctably into the evangelical anti-slavery camp even if that ran the risk of provoking social convulsion.

Roland Delattre says, plausibly if a little unexpectedly, that Edwards would have been comfortable in the company of Jim Wallis, Abraham Joshua Heschel, and Martin Luther King Jr. The statement is unexpected because these are men of the modern political left whom one does not instantly associate with Jonathan Edwards. The statement is plausible, however, because opposing slavery, like opposing the iniquities of wealth, would represent a logical extension of Edwards's insistence on charity and the oneness of humanity—in which case one might invite Frederick Douglass into the company as well. All of which reinforces John Smith's contention that Edwards had an institutional as well as an individualistic orientation: "Evil and corruption for Edwards are not confined to individuals alone but infect institutions and all the relations that make up society. It is for this reason that overcoming the ills of a social order cannot be accomplished merely by the transformation of individuals one at a time."[9]

None of this erases the received Edwards personae. He remains a scold, though chiefly of self-centeredness and selfishness. He remains a seminal figure in the evolution of revivalism, though revival guided by intellect and in the service of ethical as well as spiritual improvement, the one ever emblematic of the other. He remains a Calvinist, but one whose doctrine is so attenuated by covenant theology, preparationism, and hope for the Millennium that it becomes all but irrelevant except as a theological construct and an inducement to a sense of unworthiness. He remains an intellectual, more rooted in Scripture than was thought a few decades ago but ever questing, avid for new arguments and evidence, absorbing modern ideas, and powerfully inventive in reading God's nature and purpose.

The ravishing tropes, by contrast, are perhaps even more full of significance, as we note how the harmony of nature and the human hand and brain play out for Edwards in the social order; how the beauty of the Godhead touches and informs human relationships; how light not only changes hearts but illuminates the path to love and holiness; and how community and grace are alike sweet to the taste.

On the matter of Edwards's image, shaped as it largely is by a single brutal sermon, it may be worth spending a final moment with his actual image, the widely reproduced portrait that Joseph Badger painted of him in the early 1750s. This is the only visual likeness we have, and it has served as the model for later depictions. What we make of the portrait has some indirect bearing on how we perceive the man. Thus Stephen Stein, a leading Edwards scholar who characterizes the Edwards of the Badger portrait as a "resolute man of God" possessed of an "unsoftened" sort of "severity" from whom a smile is "an unthinkable prospect."[10]

The Badger painting, now at Yale University, is a bust portrait of a bewigged Edwards in a black robe with white clerical collar and tabs of the type commonly worn in eighteenth-century New England ministerial portraiture. The wig and collar frame a longish face with a slender but noticeable chin that thrusts slightly outward. A yellowish-brown light washes across the face from Edwards's left front, leaving the bare background dark above his right shoulder but brightly illuminated behind his left shoulder in nearly the same hue as the face. Collar, face, wig, and background thus form a tight dramatic cluster that fixes the viewer's eye.

One reason for this is that Edwards's face seems very smooth, even bleached out, not at all the face of the gaunt, ill forty-eight-year-old man described by acquaintances. The high forehead is completely unlined, giving Edwards an unlikely onion-like dome beneath his wig. There are no lines of any kind from the corners of the mouth to the edges of the nose, where one would expect them in a sickly hard-working individual who has just lost his job. There are, possibly in compensation, barely perceptible shadows at the corners of the mouth. The mouth itself is small and thin-lipped, with the lips curiously reddish, as though just touched with rouge, though more probably they are simply touched by Badger's brush. The mouth does not exactly promise a smile, but at the farthest corners is perhaps the barest hint of a turn upward.

The other reason, besides lighting and formal composition, why the portrait seems dramatic is beyond a doubt Edwards's eyes, which are open wide and show large pupils just tipped with white highlight and staring, as though unblinking and unwavering, directly into the viewer's own eyes. The gaze is piercing, seeming to penetrate the viewer's private self, if not indeed the viewer's soul. The effect is not only dramatic but vaguely unnerving. In the black and white photograph of the portrait that appears in many books, the effect is, if anything, even more pronounced.

Reading the portrait as severe and unsmiling may be unfair. In their portraits, the great divines of early New England on whom Edwards modeled himself seldom smiled. Portraits of other mid-eighteenth-century ministers, including John Lowell, Jonathan Mayhew, and Charles Chauncy, all theological liberals, show neither smile nor inclination to smile. Being liked was not a particular virtue in America until quite recently, and certainly not among these men. God did not put them on the earth to be liked.

Likewise, a harsh reading fails to consider timing. Edwards had just been turned out of his living and was in poor health, so that if he appears severe he had reason enough. Badger's preternaturally unlined depiction does not of course capture this, although Edwards would surely not have wanted him to. Edwards's gauntness alone may make him seem severe. Portraits of eighteenth-century ministers from urban pulpits often show generally fleshier faces suggestive of ample dining and a certain conviviality, thus confirming the stereotype about rotundity and cheerfulness that runs from Shakespeare to the twentieth century. Badger's Edwards looks a little more like a seventeenth-century than an eighteenth-century figure—more Richard or Increase Mather, perhaps, than Cotton.[11]

The ministers in some colonial portraits, moreover, fairly radiate hauteur and loftiness, the kind of pride and self-satisfaction that merchant portraits of the period show and that painters sometimes highlighted with backgrounds showing leather-bound books, lavish curtains or carpets, or estate backdrops.[12] There is none of this in the Badger portrait of Edwards, which seems in this respect among the most straight-forward and unpretentious of the period.

What about those startling eyes? Joseph Badger painted Edwards's eyes the same way he painted the eyes of many of the other subjects of his surviving portraits, whether ministers, merchants, women, or children: open very wide and with a frontal stare and highlighted pupils. Eyes were a problem for other early American portraitists, but none had quite as much difficulty with them as Badger, probably the least talented of the New England painters active before the 1760s. Badger, the self-taught son of a Boston tailor, worked exclusively in Boston according to conservative formulae and pieced together a living painting houses and signage as well as people. One of his better pictures may have been his portrait of Sarah Edwards, but even here, where he handles the long dark hair and translucent ruffled trim of the neckline well, the eyes are just wrong— precisely those of Jonathan and everyone else. For another example, see Badger's portrait of George Whitefield in wig, gown, and collar. The dominant feature is Whitefield's most prominent feature, his wide, staring—crossed—eyes. Even in a rather good portrait of John Adams done in 1753, Badger includes, besides a fine wig and dazzling waistcoat, those same round eerily staring eyes. He includes them as well in a "Portrait of Two Children" (1760) and in all three mid-century portraits on display at the Worcester Art Museum. Edwards's piercing eyes are not really his own. They are Joseph Badger's.[13]

Another important image of Edwards has also cast its spell through countless photographic reproductions. This is the bronze bas-relief of Edwards that hangs on the right wall of the sanctuary of the First Churches of Northampton, which occupies the site of Edwards's original church. Crafted by Herbert Adams and unveiled in 1900, exactly 150 years after Edwards's dismissal, the bas-relief catches much of the conventional wisdom—the high forehead of the aloof intellectual, the judging eyes of the fearsome preacher, the lofty bewigged unapproachable man of God. When the congregation comes into the sanctuary for Sunday service, members drift almost always to the left side, away from the formidable visage on the wall. There are doubtless many reasons for this. But it seems likely they are resistant, if only subconsciously, to experiencing the stare of a figure who perhaps seems ready to scold them. As well he might, should he come suddenly to life.

But the sculpture is misleading, just as the Badger portrait is misleading. It's actually the way the bas-relief is lighted and the deep cuts Adams uses to capture the likeness that make the eyes appear dark and glowering and judgmental and the visage stern and lofty. The impression is not exactly wrong. It simply exaggerates certain features at the expense of others, such as the open and inviting right hand at the lower left reaching out as though to touch us. The real Jonathan Edwards, the Edwards of "Heaven Is a World of Love" as well as "Sinners in the Hands of an Angry God," is like the wall sculpture. It's the lighting that history has thrown on him that makes him seem so daunting. If you look closely, you see not only the shadowy judging eyes but also the loving hand.

Abbreviations

The following volumes of *The Works of Jonathan Edwards,* published by Yale University Press, are cited in the notes as *Works* followed by the volume and page number. Where the editor's name precedes the citation, the reference is to an editorial comment, headnote, or introduction.

2 John E. Smith, ed. *Religious Affections.* 1959.

3 Clyde A. Holbrook, ed. *Original Sin.* 1970.

5 Stephen Stein, ed. *Apocalyptic Writings.* 1977.

7 Norman Pettit, ed. *The Life of David Brainerd.* 1985.

8 Paul Ramsey, ed. *Ethical Writings.* 1989.

9 John F. Wilson, ed. *A History of the Work of Redemption.* 1989.

10 Wilson Kimnach, ed. *Sermons and Discourses, 1720–1723.* 1992.

11 Wallace E. Anderson and Mason I. Lowance, Jr., with David Watters, eds. *Typological Writings.* 1993.

13 Thomas A. Schafer, ed. *The "Miscellanies" a–z, aa–zz, 1–500.* 1994.

14 Kenneth P. Minkema, ed. *Sermons and Discourses, 1723–1729.* 1997.

15 Stephen Stein, ed. *Notes on Scripture.* 1998.

16 George S. Claghorn, ed. *Letters and Personal Writings.* 1998.

17 Mark Valeri, ed. *Sermons and Discourses, 1730–1733.* 1999.

18 Ava Chamberlain, ed. *The "Miscellanies" 501–832.* 2000.

19 M. X. Lesser, ed. *Sermons and Discourses, 1734–1738.* 2001.

20 Amy Plantinga Pauw, ed. *The "Miscellanies" 833–1152.* 2002.

21 Sang Hyun Lee, ed. *Writings on the Trinity, Grace, and Faith.* 2003.

22 Harry S. Stout and Nathan O. Hatch, with Kyle P. Farley, eds. *Sermons and Discourses, 1739–1742.* 2003.

23 Douglas A. Sweeney, ed. *The "Miscellanies" 1153–1360.* 2004.

24 Stephen Stein, ed. *The Blank Bible.* 2005.

25 Wilson Kimnach, ed. *Sermons and Discourses, 1743–1758.* 2006.

26 Peter J. Thuesen, ed. *Catalogue of Books.* 2008.

Notes

1. Life

1. Biographical details are from George Marsden, *Jonathan Edwards, A Life* (New Haven: Yale University Press, 2003); Patricia Tracy, *Jonathan Edwards, Pastor* (New York: Hill and Wang, 1979); Ola Elizabeth Winslow, *Jonathan Edwards, 1703–1758: A Life* (New York: Macmillan, 1941); Iain H. Murray, *Jonathan Edwards, A New Biography* (Carlisle: Banner of Truth Trust, 1987); Kenneth P. Minkema, comp., "A Chronology of Edwards's Life and Writings," Yale Center for Jonathan Edwards Studies; "Important Dates in the Life of Edwards," in Gerald R. McDermott, ed., *Understanding Jonathan Edwards: An Introduction to America's Theologian* (Oxford: Oxford University Press, 2009), xv–xvii; Stephen J. Stein, ed., *The Cambridge Companion to Jonathan Edwards* (Cambridge: Cambridge University Press, 2007), xvii–xviii; and scattered other sources.

2. Personae

1. Murray, *Edwards,* xix; Richard A. S. Hall, "The Historical Background to the Edwards Tercentenary," in Hall, ed., *The Contribution of Jonathan Edwards to American Culture and Society* (Lewiston: Edwin Mellen Press, 2008), 3–27; John Opie in Opie, ed., *Jonathan Edwards and the Enlightenment* (New York: D. C. Heath, 1969), v.

2. Donald Weber, "Introduction," Perry Miller, *Jonathan Edwards* (Amherst: University of Massachusetts edition, 1981), xxiv.

3. Marsden, *Edwards,* 65–67.

4. Cf. Hall, "The Historical Background," in Hall, *Contribution,* 8–11.

5. Quoted in Marsden, *Edwards,* 67.

6. Clyde A. Holbrook, *The Ethics of Jonathan Edwards* (Ann Arbor: Michigan, 1973), vi: Murray, *Edwards,* 291–98 and passim; Peter Theusen in *Works* 26:21–24, 34–35, 51, 61, 75, 91.

7. Thuesen in *Works* 26:75.

8. Raymond Phineas Stearns quoted in Thuesen in *Works* 26:94. Some scholars note, correctly, that Edwards was an opponent of unadulterated Lockean empiricism, which would preclude knowledge through the influx of grace. See e.g. James Hoopes, "Calvinism and Consciousness from Edwards to Beecher," in Nathan O. Hatch and Harry S. Stout, eds., *Jonathan Edwards and the American Experience* (Oxford: Oxford University Press, 1988), 209.

9. *Works* 8:550–55; 17:67. The "God-entranced" label is John Piper's, quoted in McDermott, *Understanding,* 6.

10. Douglas Sweeney, "Jonathan Edwards and the Bible," in McDermott, *Understanding,* 68; Wolter H. Rose, "Alternative Viewpoint: Edwards and the Bible," in ibid., 87. Paul Ramsey points out that in the pre-modern era Christian theological language was "not set against metaphysical language, or biblical against theological." Ramsey in *Works* 8:32.

11. M. X. Lesser in *Works* 19:14.

12. Cf. John E. Smith, *Jonathan Edwards* (South Bend: Notre Dame, 1992), 99; Stephen J. Stein, "Edwards as biblical exegete," in Stein, *Cambridge Companion*, 184–86 and passim.

13. On the basics of typology, see e.g. Sacvan Bercovitch, "Introduction," Bercovitch, *Typology and Early American Literature* (Amherst: University of Massachusetts Press, 1972), 3–8.

14. Wilson Kimnach in *Works* 25:16–17; Harry S. Stout in *Works* 22:8–10 and passim; Lesser in *Works* 19:143; Mason Lowance Jr., " 'Images or Shadows of Divine Things' in the Thought of Jonathan Edwards," in Bercovitch, *Typology*, 216.

15. Stout in *Works* 22:18–22, 37–39; Lowance, "Thought of Jonathan Edwards," in Bercovitch, *Typology*, 217–18, 240–44; especially Janice Knight, "Typology," in Sang Lyun Lee, ed., *The Princeton Companion to Jonathan Edwards* (Princeton: Princeton University Press, 2005), 190–207.

16. Marsden, *Edwards*, 503–5. Miller remains the most provocative student of Edwards's relation to Locke. Miller, *Edwards*, 117–21 and passim. See Janice Knight for a mildly stated latter-day defense of Miller on Edwards and Locke. Knight, "Typology," in Lee, *Princeton Companion*, 192–95.

17. F. J. Woodbridge, quoted in Murray, *Edwards*, xx; Marsden, *Edwards*, 4; Tracy, *Edwards*, 11; Kenneth Minkema in *Works* 17:3.

18. Quoted in Mark Valeri in *Works* 14:3.

19. Holbrook, *Ethics*, 6.

20. *Works* 8:550–51.

21. *Works* 19:805.

22. McDermott, *Understanding*, 8; Holbrook, *Ethics*, 3–4.

23. Quoted in Holbrook, *Ethics*, 2.

24. *Works* 14:82–83, 148–49; 21:134, 147.

25. *Works* 15:56.

26. *Works* 15:63, 314.

27. *Works* 15:341.

28. *Works* 15:205; Sweeney, "Edwards and the Bible," in McDermott, *Understanding*, 77; Stein, "Eschatology," in Lee, *Princeton Companion*, 228; Gerald R. McDermott, "Missions and Native Americans," ibid., 269; Harry S. Stout, "The Puritans and Edwards," ibid., 286–87. Virtually all of Edwards's anti-Catholic imagery may be found in the Book of Revelation.

29. *Works* 13:195–96; Stein in *Works* 15:67, 89. Stephen Stein, though accepting that Edwards agreed with a 2000 date for the arrival of the Millennium at a particular time in his life, provides useful details on his shifting hopes for the dawning of the period that would eventually usher in the Millennium. Stein, "Eschatology," in Lee, *Princeton Companion*, 228–35, 239.

30. Quoted in Marsden, *Edwards*, 75–76.

31. Marsden, *Edwards*, 72–75.

32. Marsden, *Edwards*, 12–13; Valeri in *Works* 17:12–13.

33. Marsden, *Edwards*, 72–76, 199. Linking doctrinal evils to Rome was always a sound polemical tactic, easy enough to do in the case of prelatical Anglicans but not unmanageable with other adversaries. A clue to why Deism and "Arminianism" so concerned Edwards may be that, as John Smith says, only one great representative of the Enlightenment, Kant, took the Reformation seriously. Smith, *Edwards*, 98.

34. Genevieve McCoy, " 'Reason for a Hope?': Evangelical Women," in Stephen J. Stein, ed., *Jonathan Edwards's Writings* (Bloomington: Indiana University Press, 1996), 182–83.

35. Marsden, *Edwards*, 335–36.

36. Quoted in Steve Studebaker, "Jonathan Edwards's Trinitarian Theology in the Context of the Early-Enlightenment Deist Controversy," in Hall, *Contribution*, 284–85.

37. Quoted in Miller, *Edwards*, 254. For more on Whitby, see Murray, *Edwards*, 283, 469.

38. Edwards himself once called divine sovereignty a "horrible doctrine," but came soon to see the "justice and reasonableness" of it. Holbrook, *Ethics*, 10. For a broader historical perspective, see Paul F. Boller Jr., *Freedom and Fate in American Thought* (Dallas: Southern Methodist University Press, 1978), 17–23 and passim.

39. Tracy, *Edwards*, 6.

40. William Breitenbach, "Edwards and the New Divinity," in Hatch and Stout, *Edwards and the American Experience*, 188.

41. Miller, *Edwards*, ix, 328; Marsden, *Edwards*, 500.

42. Winslow, *Edwards*, 326–27, 329. For a concise assessment of how Edwards's Calvinist theology fared in the next three generations, see James Hoopes, "Calvinism and Consciousness from Edwards to Beecher," in Hatch and Stout, *Edwards and the American Experience*, 205–9.

43. Weber in Miller, *Edwards*, xvi; Marsden, *Edwards*, 4; Opie, "Introduction," v; Samuel Eliot Morison, *Three Centuries of Harvard* (Cambridge: Harvard University Press, 1936), 165–87, 218–20; Ronald Story, *The Forging of an Aristocracy* (Wesleyan: Wesleyan University Press, 1980), 91–92.

44. *Works* 19:801.

45. Quoted in Murray, *Edwards*, 115–16.

46. Tracy, *Edwards*, 110–11 and passim; Kimnach in *Works* 10:13.

47. Cf. Holbrook, *Ethics*, 24, 37. Holbrook calls this alternation a crass form of utilitarianism.

48. Quoted in Tracy, *Edwards*, 116–17. This account follows Tracy.

49. Quoted in Murray, *Edwards*, 118, 122.

50. Joseph Conforti, *Jonathan Edwards, Religious Tradition, and American Culture* (Chapel Hill: University of North Carolina Press, 1995), 23–30, 46–56.

51. Murray, *Edwards*, 155–76; Laura Broderick Ricard, "The Evangelical New Light Clergy of Northern New England, 1741–1755: A Typology" (doctoral diss., New Hampshire, 1985); Harry S. Stout, "Edwards and Revival," in McDermott, *Understanding*, 45.

52. Tracy, *Edwards*, 31; Kimnach in *Works* 10:15; Stout in *Works* 22:33ff. Edwards's father, Timothy Edwards, in Connecticut, agreed with Stoddard on the need for such preaching. Marsden, *Edwards*, 58.

53. Stout in *Works* 22:401; Miller, *Edwards*, 145–46 and passim.

54. J. A. Leo Lemay quoted in Stout in *Works* 22:401.

55. Holbrook, *Ethics*, 30–31; Marsden, *Edwards*, 220–24; Winslow, *Edwards*, 193. Probably the best overview of the Awakening remains Alan Heimert and Perry Miller, "Introduction," in Heimert and Miller, eds., *The Great Awakening* (Minneapolis: Bobbs-Merrill, 1967), xiii–lxiii, although this places possibly too great emphasis on the Awakening's class dimension and its resemblance to the political enthusiasm of the Revolution. Edwards would probably have supported declaring independence from Britain out of hostility to British corruption and the threat to colonial religion, among other things, but would have, I'm fairly sure, loathed the bitterness and vituperation of the Revolution itself.

56. Lesser in *Works* 19:7.

57. Cf. Valeri in *Works* 17:8–9, 36–37.

58. On this interesting point, see e.g. Willem van Vlastuin, "Alternative Viewpoint: Edwards and Revival," in McDermott, *Understanding*, 59.

59. Marsden, *Edwards*, 280, 282; Van Vlastuin, "Alternative Viewpoint," in McDermott, *Understanding*, 58.

60. Quoted in Norman Pettit in *Works* 7:93.

61. Marsden, *Edwards*, 269–78. On the behavior of the New Light radicals, see e.g. Ri-

card, "Evangelical New Light Clergy," 57–70. Edwards especially abhorred the censorious behavior of some "zealous friends of this glorious work of God," with their "heat" and anger and insistence on public displays of enthusism, so unlike the behavior of Jesus Christ himself. Jonathan Edwards, *Select Works* (Carlisle: Banner of Truth Trust) I:141–46.

62. Every student of colonial New England religion discusses the covenant. The foundation text is Perry Miller, *The New England Mind: The 17th Century* (New York: Macmillan, 1939), but see also Miller, *Edwards*, 209–13; Gerald R. McDermott, *One Holy and Happy Society* (University Park: Pennsylvania State University Press, 1992), 11ff.; Harry S. Stout, "The Puritans and Edwards," in Hatch and Stout, *Edwards and the American Experience*, 143–56.

63. For the phenomenon of jeremiad preaching, together with sharp criticism of Edwards, see Sacvan Bercovitch, *The Puritan Jeremiad* (Cambridge: Harvard University Press, 1978).

64. Quoted in Winslow. *Edwards*, 227. For a useful overview of Edwards and the ministry, see Helen Westra, *The Minister's Task and Calling in the Sermons of Jonathan Edwards* (Lewiston: Edwin Mellen Press, 1986).

65. *Works* 14:216–18, 222–23, 227.

66. *Works* 17:93, 96–98, 100.

67. Titles with approximate dates are in appendices in *Works* 14, 17, 19, 22, 25.

68. *Works* 14:485.

69. *Works* 19:18–19, 28–29, 354.

70. McDermott, *One Holy,* 22–23.

71. Winslow, *Edwards,* 171.

72. Tracy, *Edwards,* 126.

73. Quoted in Tracy, *Edwards,* 128–31.

74. Cf. Ricard, "New Light Clergy," 253–58 and passim.

75. Winslow, *Edwards,* 215–19; Tracy, *Edwards,* 157–60; Murray, *Edwards.* 277–81; *Works* 25:59–102. Slaves, all African, were owned for life and could own no property without permission; their children commonly, though not always as yet, inherited their condition; the Edwards family both bought and sold slaves, though infrequently. Servants, nearly all European, were either bound by indentures until their release into freedom or worked for wages in money or kind. Few indentured servants remained in Massachusetts Bay by the mid-18th century, so that the Edwards servants were likely wage workers. The treatment of slaves and servants was often very similar, in some cases considerate and in others not.

76. Every biography covers this affair. Patricia Tracy's treatment is particularly insightful and sensitive. Tracy, *Edwards,* 160–66.

77. Marsden, *Edwards,* 260–62, 346–48; Tracy, *Edwards,* 154–55, 169–71, passim. Stoddard's practice was actually inconsistent on access to the sacraments, changing directions more than once, though hardly any of Edwards's parishioners would have remembered that. Paul R. Lucas, *Valley of Discord* (Lebanon: University Press of New England, 1976), 150ff.

78. Marsden, *Edwards,* 227, 368–70, 373; Winslow, *Edwards,* 327–28; Tracy, *Edwards,* 188.

79. *Works* 25:678–79.

3. Tropes

1. See e.g. Marsden, *Edwards,* 5–6; Winslow, *Edwards,* 66–67, 132–33, 227; Tracy, *Edwards,* 109, 147; Stein in Stein, *Cambridge Companion,* 1–14. One does find the occasional soupçon of wit, but humor was not a strong suit.

2. Harry S. Stout, "Edwards and Revival," in McDermott, *Understanding,* 49; Murray,

Edwards, 178, 329.

3. Murray, *Edwards,* 180–86. Summaries of Hopkins's and others' recollections appear in most biographies. Cf. Marsden, *Edwards,* 133–36, 249–56; Winslow, *Edwards,* 130–34.

4. Miller, *Edwards,* 225; Murray, *Edwards,* 328–29.

5. Marsden, *Edwards,* 432.

6. Cf. Stout in *Works* 22:402–3; Stout, "Edwards and Revival," in McDermott, *Understanding,* 48–50; Van Vlastuin, "Alternative Viewpoint," in ibid., 54.

7. Kimnach in *Works* 10:223; Marsden, *Edwards,* 55.

8. *Works* 8:530–31.

9. *Works* 13:434–35.

10. *Works* 5:384; 15:227.

11. *Works* 15:214, 216.

12. *Works* 25:707–8; 21:132, 264.

13. Valeri in *Works* 17:40; *Works* 21:119.

14. *Works* 21:119.

15. *Works* 17:154.

16. Quoted in Douglas A. Sweeney, "Edwards and the Bible," in McDermott, *Understanding,* 69.

17. *Works* 21:120–21.

18. *Works* 15:148; 11:287.

19. *Works* 15:148–49.

20. *Works* 15:214–17.

21. Quoted in Valeri in *Works* 17:43.

22. Quoted in Anna Svetlikova, "Alternative Viewpoint: The Literary Life," in McDermott, *Understanding,* 149.

23. *Works* 15:303.

24. Quoted in Marsden, *Edwards,* 550.

25. *Works* 11:85.

26. *Works* 11:121.

27. *Works* 11:52.

28. *Works* 17:325–27.

29. Quoted in Lesser in *Works* 19:16.

30. *Works* 21:160.

31. *Works* 11:101, 135; 17:328; 15:226–27, 290–91.

32. *Works* 21:118, 242; quoted in Marsden, *Edwards,* 59, 444.

33. *Works* 25:108.

34. *Works* 15:303; 5:384.

35. *Works* 11:90; Marsden, *Edwards,* 5.

36. *Works* 15:142.

37. Quoted in Marsden, *Edwards,* 162. See also Scott D. Seay, "Satan and his *Maleficium* in the Thought of Jonathan Edwards," in Hall, *Contribution,* 266–67; Edwards, *Select Works* I:110.

38. *Works* 21:139.

39. *Works* 15:225.

40. *Works* 15:330–31.

41. *Works* 15:332–35.

42. *Works* 25:91–93, 96–97, 99. See also *Works* 15:320–21; Murray, *Edwards,* 144.

43. Kimnach in *Works* 10:199.

44. Roland Andre Delattre, "Beauty and Theology: A Reappraisal of Jonathan Edwards," in William J. Scheick, ed., *Critical Essays on Jonathan Edwards* (Boston: G. K. Hall, 1980), 136–37.

45. Tibor Fabiny, "Edwards and Biblical Typology," in McDermott, *Understanding*, 94.

46. For the equivalence of beauty and excellence, see e.g. *Works* 8:550; Sang Hyun Lee in *Works* 21:1–108; Miller, *Edwards*, 192. See also Minkema in *Works* 17:6 ("excellency, beauty, and harmony"); Kimnach in *Works* 10:202 ("the knowledge and experience of beauty (Excellence)"); Fabiny, "Edwards and Biblical Typology," in McDermott, *Understanding*, 92 ("excellency means beauty"). Herbert Richardson similarly highlights excellency as a synonym for beauty. Richardson, "Why Is Jonathan Edwards America's Spiritual Founding Father?" in Hall, *Contribution*, 69.

47. *Works* 8:561–62.

48. *Works* 2:365.

49. *Works* 8:568.

50. Holbrook, *Ethics*, 167.

51. Quoted in Anderson in *Works* 6:7; *Works* 6:335. Edwards penned these recollections in 1739.

52. *Works* 6:305.

53. Quoted in Winslow, *Edwards*, 139.

54. *Works* 11:56.

55. *Works* 8:562–67.

56. *Works* 15:245, 613; 19:83; 10:202, 479, 539, 613; 25:103–6, 633, 635–36, 705; 13:329–31; Kenneth P. Minkema, "Personal Writings," in Stein, *Cambridge Companion*, 42.

57. *Works* 6:305–6.

58. *Works* 8:567.

59. *Works* 6:304–7; 11:276.

60. *Works* 13:329.

61. *Works* 25:636; 8:619; 13:329.

62. *Works* 13:305–6.

63. *Works* 13:330–32.

64. Marsden, *Edwards*, 99.

65. Quoted in Marsden, *Edwards*, 94.

66. *Works* 13:278–79.

67. *Works* 8:36; 6:305.

68. *Works* 8:564–65.

69. *Works* 13:278–79, 330.

70. Quoted in Miller, *Edwards*, 235.

71. Quoted in Holbrook, *Ethics*, 166.

72. *Works* 8:550–51.

73. *Works* 8:550–51; 10:478–79.

74. *Works* 25:636.

75. Ramsey in *Works* 8:701.

76. E. Brooks Holifield, "Edwards as Theologian," in Stein, *Cambridge Companion*, 149.

77. Quoted ibid., 155.

78. Cf. *Works* 8:573. Holbrook, however, calls beauty "the surrogate of true virtue," as does Roland Delattre at greater length. Holbrook, *Ethics*, 167; Roland Delattre, "Religious Ethics Today: Jonathan Edwards, H. Richard Niebuhr, and Beyond," in Sang Hyun Lee and Allen C. Guelzo, eds., *Edwards in Our Time: Jonathan Edwards and the Shaping of American Religion* (Grand Rapids: Eerdmans, 1999), 67–86.

79. *Works* 11:81.

80. *Works* 13:356; Ramsey in *Works* 8:700; Sweeney, "Edwards and the Bible," in McDermott, *Understanding*, 69.

81. Quoted in Marsden, *Edwards*, 78.

82. *Works* 6:93.

83. *Works* 11:35, 97.

84. *Works* 8:539.

85. *Works* 26:94–95.

86. *Works* 11:336.

87. *Works* 6:336–37; 11:81.

88. *Works* 11:96–97.

89. *Works* 6:93.

90. Sweeney, "Edwards and the Bible," in McDermott, *Understanding,* 69.

91. McDermott, *One Holy,* 67; *Works* 9:484.

92. *Works* 13:216; Murray, *Edwards,* 141.

93. Sweeney, "Edwards and the Bible," in McDermott, *Understanding,* 67; Stein in *Works* 15:29.

94. *Works* 23:7.

95. *Works* 11:212–13.

96. *Works* 15:77.

97. *Works* 11:264.

98. *Works* 15:77.

99. Murray, *Edwards,* 187; Kimnach in *Works* 10:224; Marsden, *Edwards,* 79, 245; *Works* 13:303.

100. *Works* 8:566.

101. *Works* 13:298, 328–31.

102. Winslow, *Edwards,* 107–8; Murray, *Edwards,* 187.

103. Marsden, *Edwards,* 144–45, 493. Peter Thuesen notes Edwards's admiration for Watts's hymns and devotional works as well as his popular books on astronomy. Watts corresponded regularly with Mather and welcomed Boston visitors to England. Thuesen in *Works* 26:54.

104. *Works* 4:151; Marsden, *Edwards,* 156; Valeri in *Works* 17:16; Lesser in *Works* 19:24.

105. *Works* 6:81.

106. *Works* 11:53; Anderson in *Works* 6:81.

107. *Works* 8:561–62.

108. Sang Hyun Lee in *Works* 21:8–11. See, however, Stephen R. Holmes, "Does Jonathan Edwards Use a Dispositional Ontology? A Response to Sang Hyun Lee," in Paul Helm and Oliver D. Crisp, eds., *Jonathan Edwards, Philosophical Theologian* (Aldershot: Ashgate, 2003), 99–114.

109. *Works* 13:96, 221, 284. Cf. Studebaker, "Jonathan Edwards' Trinitarian Theology," in Hall, *Contribution,* 281–301; Amy Plantinga Pauw, "'One Alone Cannot Be Excellent': Edwards on Divine Simplicity," in Helm and Crisp, *Jonathan Edwards,* 115–25.

110. *Works* 8:540.

111. *Works* 13:296.

112. Quoted in Marsden, *Edwards,* 78.

113. Richardson, "Why Is Jonathan Edwards America's Spiritual Founding Father?" in Hall, *Contribution,* 69.

114. *Works* 19:439–49.

115. *Works* 14:101–6.

116. *Works* 8:619.

117. Cf. *Works* 6:346ff.

118. *Works* 14:102–8.

119. *Works* 13:163, 176, 221, 260–63, 281, 290–96.

120. Quoted in Daniel B. Shea, "The Art and Instruction of Jonathan Edwards' Personal Narrative," in Scheick, *Critical Essays,* 272; and in Kenneth Minkema in *Works* 17:4.

121. *Works* 16:793–800.

122. Wayne Lesser, "Jonathan Edwards: Textuality and the Language of Man," in Scheick, *Critical Essays,* 298–303.

123. *Works* 19:82–85.

124. *Works* 19:83–84; cf. also 13:218–19.

125. *Works* 14:101–13.

126. *Works* 11:52.

127. *Works* 14:104–12.

128. *Works* 19:449, 461; 20:66, 183, 217, 232.

129. *Works* 25:180.

130. *Works* 14:103–9.

131. *Works* 11:313.

132. *Works* 19:463.

133. *Works* 17:130–35. The whale swallowed Jonah as a "sweet feast," Edwards recounts in another harmonizing of Old and New Testaments, only to "vomit him up" like dreadful medicine in three days; the devil, thinking Christ was his food, freed him from the tomb likewise in three days. This is an example of Edwards's wry humor in the pulpit. There were a few. *Works* 15:78ff.

134. For Brainerd's life and labors and the Brainerd-Edwards relationship, cf. Norman Pettit in *Works* 7:1–71; Marsden, *Edwards.*

135. *Works* 7:142–48, 158–65, 177 and e.g. 200, 227, 229–35, 246, 270.

136. *Works* 7:200, 227, 234, 246, 504, 509.

4. Charity

1. *Works* 14:175.

2. Stout, "The Puritans and Edwards," in Hatch and Stout, *Edwards and the American Experience,* 11. For a thorough airing of the covenant concept, see Edwards's sermon from April 1738 on a text from Jeremiah. Sermon 468, WJE Online, Jonathan Edwards Center.

3. *Works* 8:40; 18:164. See Ramsey in *Works* 8:72–73; Minkema in *Works* 14:213; Marsden, *Edwards,* 138–39.

4. *Works* 13:282. Scholars have written extensively about the covenant and the nature of conversion because after the Reformation and the settling of New England, ministers and divines themselves wrote extensively about these subjects, which were the chief means to differentiate Reformed and Roman Catholic Christianity. See e.g. Minkema in *Works* 14:50; Valeri in *Works* 17:9–12; Stout, "Puritans and Edwards," in Hatch and Stout, *Edwards and the American Experience,* 142–51.

5. *Works* 2:452–53. Cf. McDermott, *Understanding,* 210.

6. *Works* 9:308.

7. *Works* 13:418.

8. *Works* 22:142.

9. William Breitenbach, "Piety and Moralism: Edwards and the New Divinity," in Hatch and Stout, *Edwards and the American Experience,* 188.

10. *Works* 19:117.

11. See e.g. *Works* 17:288, 302–3. Note that Edwards used the word "lust" for any obsessive worldly longing, not just physical or sexual desire, which was in conformity with Paul in the book of Romans and much other traditional early Christian usage. See e.g. Richard B. Steele, *"Gracious Affection" and "True Virtue" According to Jonathan Edwards and John Wesley* (Lanham: Scarecrow, 1994), 38–39.

12. *Works* 19:626–27.

13. *Works* 2:387, 419; 8:333; 14:263; 15:277–27.

14. *Works* 6:338.

15. *Works* 15:7; 8:180.

16. *Works* 22:130, 152.

17. *Works* 8:151.

18. *Works* 21:473, 490–91.

19. *Works* 8:129.

20. *Works* 19:626–27.

21. *Works* 17:300.

22. *Works* 24:909.

23. *Works* 13:416; 8:180.

24. *Works* 22:71, 260.

25. *Works* 2:254–55.

26. *Works* 10:561–62.

27. *Works* 10:345.

28. *Works* 14:258–59, 268.

29. *Works* 14:238–41, 260, 547.

30. *Works* 17:110–11, 250, 289, 433.

31. Edwards, *Select Works* I:148.

32. *Works* 17:372–76.

33. *Works* 17:376–87.

34. Valeri in *Works* 17:369.

35. *Works* 17:390–94.

36. *Works* 17:395–98.

37. *Works* 17:398–400.

38. *Works* 17:400–401.

39. *Works* 17:402–4.

40. *Works* 24:474, 1045.

41. *Works* 17:298–99.

42. *Works* 10:502.

43. *Works* 22:75.

44. *Works* 19:626–27; 24:167; 17:300; 21:491; 18:527.

45. *Works* 9:300–330; 14:546.

46. *Works* 18:59; 2:385; 22:385. Cf. Fabiny, "Edwards and Biblical Typology," in McDermott, *Understanding*, 92–93.

47. *Works* 24:686–87.

48. *Works* 9:494. In 1774 this series of sermons would be published as *A History of the Work of Redemption*.

49. Cf. e.g. *Works* 24:1196.

50. *Works* 19:626–27; 22:385.

51. *Works* 17:409; 13:507; 23:324.

52. *Works* 17:265; 24:53, 1050; 8:175.

53. *Works* 15:316–17.

54. *Works* 9:367.

55. *Works* 18:55–57; 19:626–27; McDermott, *One Holy*, 93–116.

56. *Works* 2:305; 9:419–20.

57. *Works* 2:336–38.

58. *Works* 22:256.

59. *Works* 19:252–54; 22:78, 379; Sermon 708, WJE Online Vol. 61, Jonathan Edwards Center; Mark Valeri, "The Economic Thought of Jonathan Edwards," *Church History* (March 1991), 46.

60. Sermon 579a, WJE Online Vol. 56, Jonathan Edwards Center.

61. *Works* 22:391.

62. *Works* 17:314, 362.

63. Amy Schrager Lang, "'A Flood of Errors': Chauncy and Edwards in the Great Awakening," in Hatch and Stout, *Edwards and the American Experience,* 168–69. The Chauncy quote is in Miller, *Edwards,* 173.

64. *Works* 12:570. For brief comments on the local reception of Edwards's written defense, see Murray, *Edwards,* 320–21.

65. Marsden, *Edwards,* 360–61.

66. *Works* 24:843, 862, 900–901.

67. *Works* 13:283, 404–5.

68. Cited in Tracy, *Edwards,* 247.

69. *Works* 2:284.

70. Edwards, *Select Works* I:66.

71. *Works* 2:337–38.

72. *Works* 22:268; 24:870; 2:369.

73. *Works* 2:370.

74. *Works* 14:491.

75. *Works* 8:187–88; 22:155, 220; 24:871.

76. *Works* 9:341.

77. Sermon 557, pp. 26–29, WJE Online Vol. 55, Jonathan Edwards Center.

78. *Works* 10:561–62.

79. *Works* 10:356.

80. Quoted in Holbrook, *Ethics,* 33; in Valeri in *Works* 17:31; in Kimnach in *Works* 25:24; in Minkema in *Works* 14:37.

81. *Works* 9:341, 484.

82. *Works* 14:504–5.

83. *Works* 3:153–54.

84. *Works* 22:219; Sermon 579a, WJE Online Vol. 56, Jonathan Edwards Center.

85. *Works* 14:86.

86. *Works* 17:92.

87. *Works* 24:884.

88. *Works* 2:432.

89. *Works* 24:1130, 1167.

90. *Works* 17:265.

91. *Works* 2:424; 19:502.

92. *Works* 19:745–46.

93. Sermon 579a, WJE Online Vol. 56, Jonathan Edwards Center.

94. Edwards, *Select Works* I:154–58; Miller, *Edwards,* 210. Harry Stout thinks this shift occurred with the waning of the Great Awakening. That too is plausible, particularly given the covenant episode discussed in the next paragraph, but it overlooks the meeting house debacle, which Edwards referenced repeatedly in his later work. Stout in *Works* 22:522.

95. Miller, *Edwards,* 210.

96. *Works* 10:341–43.

97. *Works* 10:314–15.

98. *Works* 17:266.

99. *Works* 17:440.

100. *Works* 19:624.

101. Quoted in McDermott, *One Holy,* 24.

102. *Works* 22:78.

103. Sermon 557, WJE Online Vol. 55, Jonathan Edwards Center.

104. *Works* 22:217, 392–93.

105. Sermon 708, WJE Online Vol. 61, Jonathan Edwards Center.

106. *Works* 2:369, 387.

107. McDermott, *One Holy,* 114–15; Tracy, *Edwards,* 110; Sermon 708, WJE Online Vol. 61, Jonathan Edwards Center. How good Edwards's salary was is never absolutely clear since the value of provincial currency fluctuated mightily, and some of his pay was in kind. But by the end of his tenure in Northampton, it was ample in spite of currency fluctuations.

108. Marsden, *Edwards,* 132.; Thuesen in *Works* 26:28; Ramsey in *Works* 8:96–97; *Works* 19:741. For an analogous historical figure, one might consider, among others, Harry Hopkins, a high official of great status and influence who lived well but had little personal wealth or privilege to sustain him or his family; or any faculty member of any 19th-century American college.

109. Quoted in Holbrook, *Ethics,* 79–80; *Works* 20:172; 19:159. For an interesting sociopolitical reading of sermons in the 1740s, see Richard A. S. Hall, *The Neglected Northampton Texts of Jonathan Edwards* (Carlisle: Edwin Mellen Press, 1990).

110. *Works* 9:304.

111. *Works* 13:184.

112. *Works* 16:52.

113. Sermon 557, WJE Online Vol. 55, Jonathan Edwards Center. See also Sermon 290, WJE Online, Jonathan Edwards Center.

114. *Works* 20:493.

115. Sermon 179, WJE Online, Jonathan Edwards Center; *Works* 9:484.

116. *Works* 22:106; Sermon 708, WJE Online Vol. 61, Jonathan Edwards Center.

117. Marsden, *Edwards,* 189, 259; Robert Jenson, *America's Theologian* (Oxford: Oxford University Press, 1988), 143, 54–55; *Works* 24:910. There is a mountainous literature on the economic transformation of New England and its consequences for social, cultural, and religious life. Kenneth Minkema says that the towns where Jonathan Edwards preached were "microcosms" of the New England shift from communal agrarian values to an "individualist, capitalist ethos," and argues that Edwards's sermons reflect the resulting tension. Minkema in *Works* 14:37. Other scholars pick other dates for the transformation; these picks span virtually the whole two centuries after the Puritan migration of the 1630s. The ur-text on how this transformation affected the New England weltanschaung is Richard L. Bushman, *From Puritan to Yankee: Character and the Social Order in Connecticut, 1690–1765* (Cambridge: Harvard University Press, 1967). Nearly all the evidence and arguments situating Northampton within this transformation rely on Patricia Tracy's *Jonathan Edwards,* which, given the paucity and ambiguity of the sources, may long command the field. See Valeri in *Works* 17:22 for a cogent summary that draws heavily on Tracy.

Though not contradicting the transformation thesis, Christopher Clark describes a hardscrabble Connecticut Valley economy that seems at odds with the impression left by historians who refer to "aristocrats" and "river gods." *The Roots of Rural Capitalism: Western Massachusetts, 1780–1860* (Ithaca: Cornell University Press, 1990). On the presumed economic transformation of New England, Barry Levy's recent exhaustive study of trade and labor in eastern Massachusetts townships finds no significant shift in attitudes after the late 1600s even well into the Revolutionary era. Barry Levy, *Town Born: The Political Economy of New England from Its Founding to the Revolution* (Philadelphia: University of Pennsylvania Press, 2009), 291. For a recent examination of shifting ministerial views on piety and economics, see Mark Valeri, *Heavenly Merchandize* (Princeton: Princeton University Press, 2010), which follows Valeri's argument in "Jonathan Edwards, the Edwardians, and Free Trade," in David W. Kling and Douglas A. Sweeney, eds., *Jonathan Edwards at Home and Abroad* (Columbia: University of South Carolina Press, 2003), 90–91. I myself see only slight correlation between Edwards's preaching and local socio-economic transformation since he made virtually the same points in the early 1720s that he made in the late 1740s.

118. Sermon 557, WJE Online Vol. 55, Jonathan Edwards Center.
119. *Works* 8:187.
120. *Works* 22:355.
121. Sermon 549a, WJE Online Vol. 56, Jonathan Edwards Center.
122. Quoted in Jenson, *America's Theologian,* 143.
123. *Works* 17:313.
124. *Works* 22:211, 218–19.
125. *Works* 17:315, 434–36.
126. *Works* 8:451–53.
127. *Works* 5:19; 21:458.

5. Community

1. Miller, *Edwards,* 107–20; Christopher Clark, "The Roots of Rural Capitalism," in Kerry Buckley, ed., *A Place Called Paradise: Culture and Community in Northampton, Massachusetts, 1651–2004* (Northampton: Historic Northampton, 2004), 198–16.
2. *Works* 22:71, 130, 152, 260.
3. *Works* 19:449, 461; 20:183, 217, 232; 25:180.
4. *Works* 19:463.
5. *Works* 14:103–10.
6. *Works* 8:561–62.
7. *Works* 13:96, 221, 284; 14:110. On this point see Lee in *Works* 21:8–11. The most exhaustive discussion of the Trinity in Edwards's theology is William J. Danaher Jr., *The Trinitarian Ethics of Jonathan Edwards* (Louisville: Westminster John Knox Press, 2004).
8. *Works* 8:561–62.
9. *Works* 13:330–32.
10. *Works* 18:472–73.
11. Quoted in McDermott, *One Holy,* 98–103.
12. *Works* 24:1102.
13. *Works* 14:128–29.
14. *Works* 10:289–90, 307–33, 381–96, 517, 572–84. Italics added.
15. These are powerful statements for an Englishman to make given the bloody struggles against Catholic France and Spain.
16. *Works* 14:129, 132–33.
17. *Works* 17:376.
18. Sermon 290 WJE Online, Jonathan Edwards Center.
19. *Works* 13:268; 20:171.
20. *Works* 23:350–54.
21. *Works* 18:54–55. A single sermon contains the words "friend" or "friendship" thirty times in as many manuscript pages. Lesser in *Works* 19:21. For more on friendship, a form of "philia," see e.g. Danaher, *Trinitarian Ethics,* 223.
22. *Works* 17:365.
23. *Works* 13:207.
24. *Works* 14:491, 504–5.
25. *Works* 17:363.
26. *Works* 10:289–90, 307–19, 324–33, 381–96, 517, 572, 583–84.
27. Edwards, *Select Works* I:12–14, 19–21, 40–47, 54.
28. *Works* 23:350. Robert Jenson highlights the significance of Edwards's notion of conversation in *America's Theologian,* 149, 167, and passim.
29. *Works* 19:117.
30. *Works* 16:53. Including Indians in the scope of town love is fairly startling given the

savage guerrilla warfare along the 18th-century frontier. See e.g. Marsden, *Edwards,* 3–4, 113–15, 414–16.

31. Edwards, *Select Works* I:68, 72.

32. Edwards, *Select Works* I:148–49.

33. Sermon 668, WJE Online Vol. 59, Jonathan Edwards Center.

34. *Works* 22:127–29, 212–17, 453, 510.

35. *Works* 15:369; 22:129.

36. *Works* 3:293.

37. *Works* 5:316–18, 320, 323–25.

38. *Works* 5:339–40, 365.

39. *Works* 3:293; 25:704. Stephen Stein provides a cogent account of the Concert of Prayer episode in *Works* 5:29–47. See also Marsden, *Edwards,* 335–40; Murray, *Edwards,* 292–310.

40. *Works* 8:451–53, 550–70. Cf. Hall, "Historical Background to the Edwards Tercentenary," in Hall, *Contribution,* 39. John Smith makes the cognate point that Edwards, though knowledgeable about Locke, was not a nominalist, "which is to say that he did not believe that individuals alone exist" or that mankind is the "sum" of individuals. History for Edwards was rather a process involving "corporate," not individual, entities. Smith, *Edwards,* 132.

41. Holbrook, *Ethics,* 203.

42. E. Brooks Holifield, "Edwards as Theologian," in Stein, *Cambridge Companion,* 155–56.

43. Ramsey in *Works* 8:71.

44. Willem van Vlastuin, "Alternative Viewpoint: Edwards and Revival," in McDermott, *Understanding,* 54. See also Jenson, *America's Theologian,* 142, on Edwards's commitment to building community in the world.

45. *Works* 25:637.

46. *Works* 19:345; 16:67.

47. *Works* 13:364; 17:365.

48. *Works* 17:357.

49. *Works* 10:343.

50. *Works* 10:561, 573.

51. *Works* 17:315.

52. *Works* 16:67; 22:259.

53. *Works* 17:104–11; 22:98–99.

54. *Works* 2:346.

55. *Works* 2:114.

56. *Works* 17:112–14.

57. *Works* 17:114–17. Some scholars interpret this and similar sermons as reflecting little more than aristocratic resentment against local parvenus, established landowners (and ministers) versus upstart tradesmen or aspiring farmers. See e.g. Minkema in *Works* 17:10–11; Tracy, *Edwards,* 38ff.; Murray, *Edwards,* 86–88. But there is a subtlety in Edwards on economics and also politics that interpretations along these lines fail to capture. See, as one example, his intriguing discussion of the division of powers in government, government's limited reach over ecclesiastical affairs, the legitimacy or illegitimacy of monarchs, and individual conscience and obedience to the law in *Works* 13:203–8. Edwards despairs in 1737 in a moment of depression after the meeting house debate of ever persuading his townspeople "to prevent and avoid contention." "I don't know but I have trusted too much in men"—an odd statement for an arch Calvinist who supposedly believed in the absolute depravity of humanity. He goes on to make the interesting comment that "I don't determine who they be" who whisper against their neighbors, "God knows who they are"—possibly because the damage is coming from high against low as well as low against high. Quoted in Lesser in *Works* 19:656–57.

58. *Works* 17:117–20.
59. *Works* 8:214–28.
60. *Works* 14:87.
61. *Works* 22:128.
62. *Works* 10:503; 20:208.
63. *Works* 24:1237.
64. *Works* 10:343; 14:174.
65. *Works* 9:335–37; 22:253.
66. *Works* 20:208–9; 18:164.
67. *Works* 24:978.
68. *Works* 18:391–92.
69. *Works* 19:350.
70. *Works* 14:469, 501–2.
71. *Works* 2:246; 22:394.
72. *Works* 19:350.
73. Sermon 290 WJE Online, Jonathan Edwards Center; *Works* 14:501–2.
74. *Works* 14:89.
75. *Works* 25:555. This observation derives largely from the early 18th century, not the late 18th century. Its reference point is Christian social order and solidarity, not the republican political theory that English Whigs were starting to articulate, but it does bite in possibly proto-republican directions.
76. *Works* 2:396.
77. *Works* 25:556.
78. *Works* 18:391.
79. *Works* 22:528–32.
80. *Works* 22:150–51.
81. *Works* 24:838. Edwards generally excepted himself and other ministers from this accusation. Scolding was a significant part of a preacher's duty.
82. *Works* 24:838.
83. *Works* 14:113.
84. *Works* 2:315.
85. *Works* 22:392–93, 531; quoted in Valeri in *Works* 17:34. For another formulation, see the statement by Stephen Yarbrough and John Adams that Edwards "sought to prepare sinners for accepting Christ by undermining or dismantling the belief structures supporting their sense of themselves as independent, self-determined individuals." Quoted in M. Darrol Bryant, "The Mind of Jonathan Edwards: Beyond America," in Hall, *Contribution*, 82. See also Gerald McDermott's comment that Edwards's "higher goal" was "the complete surrender of self." McDermott, *Understanding*, 23.
86. *Works* 17:307.
87. *Works* 10:502–3.
88. *Works* 21:486–89, 494, 502.
89. *Works* 24:1105.
90. *Works* 13:279–80.
91. *Works* 21:513–19.
92. *Works* 10:473. The proud, he elaborates, refuse the "spiritual humiliation" that shows the need for grace. They "despise a crucified Savior, one that suffered such disgrace, and humbled himself so low." They "make themselves enemies of Christ." Quoted in Pauw in *Works* 20:28.
93. Edwards, *Selected Works* I:45–47.
94. *Works* 18:488–91.
95. *Works* 22:256–57, 378.

96. *Works* 2:315, 346–53, 387. The evils that undermine community permeated in a curious way Edwards's dismissal in 1750, which was precipitated when he seemed to tighten the requirements for joining the church and participating in its sacraments. The ensuing arguments vividly encapsulate the long debate over Christ's injunction, like Edwards's, to Christian unity. Solomon Stoddard, as we know, had argued that the sacraments were "saving ordinances" and permitted all residents (except apparently outsiders) to approach the Lord's Table. But Edwards preached as early as 1731 that the Lord's Supper should be a sacred expression of Christian unity. It should not be the preserve of "the rich and the worthy" who might have "purchased such a blessing with money." It is in fact for everyone, including the "poor, the maimed, the halt and the blind, the naked, the filthy." It must not therefore be "polluted" by men pretending to "love and friendship" while harboring feelings of "hatred," "envy," "revenge," and "malice." *Works* 17:271–72.

He says in 1745, drawing a line in the sand and employing devastating and doubtless infuriating language, that people may partake as "friends and disciples" or as "blood thirsty cannibals." They may be in "communion with Christ," our model, or face "damnation." Five years later the congregation erupted in the kind of factional behavior that he had assailed for thirty years. The result was "contention, heat of spirit," and "evil speaking" contrary to the spirit of Christianity, and a decision by a committee of the congregation to dismiss him. It is worth noting that Joseph Hawley, a leader of the successful anti-Edwards uprising and the son of the man who committed suicide during the revival of 1735, years later published a guilt-ridden letter apologizing for his role in the dismissal. Hawley ascribed his behavior to "vast pride, self-sufficiency, ambition, and vanity." Quoted in Marsden, *Edwards,* 328, 348, 354. The symbolism of the affair, especially Hawley's apology, is striking since it was precisely these sins that led Edwards to conclude that townspeople were unworthy to take communion in the first place.

97. *Works* 20:172.

98. *Works* 18:174–75.

99. *Works* 11:224, 276–78.

100. *Works* 17:96.

101. Cf. *Works* 26:21. Norman Fiering, *Jonathan Edwards's Moral Thought and Its British Context* (Chapel Hill: University of North Carolina Press, 1981), provides exhaustive coverage of this topic.

102. *Works* 21:516–19.

103. *Works* 2:419.

6. Love

1. *Works* 8:135.

2. *Works* 2:106.

3. *Works* 21:11, 131.

4. *Works* 2:114.

5. *Works* 16:232.

6. *Works* 21:121, 186–87; 16:415. For an examination of the importance of the Trinity to the notions of love, see Danaher, *Trinitarian Ethics,* which also provides definitions, with appropriate Greek headings, of different types of love (p. 221).

7. *Works* 8:460.

8. *Works* 21:172, 194–95. Edwards sometimes uses the word "creature" rather than "man" or "human" because there are millions of other creatures dear to the divinity—namely, angels. On Edwards and angels, see e.g. Stout, "Edwards as Revivalist," in Stein, *Cambridge Companion,* 131–33.

9. *Works* 8:443; 2:116.

10. *Works* 24:1196.

11. *Works* 2:106–14, 246, 270; 24:996–97.

12. *Works* 2:262; 13:261, 390, 466.

13. *Works* 13:177.

14. *Works* 8:443. Edwards acknowledges the Holy Ghost as the principal purveyor of God's love to human souls following the atonement, but the Spirit, except during revival outpourings, receives less attention than the other two entities of the Godhead. Cf. *Works* 21:130–31.

15. *Works* 16:225.

16. *Works* 2:326.

17. *Works* 2:103.

18. *Works* 16:232.

19. *Works* 21:360.

20. *Works* 24:1197. Italics added.

21. *Works* 6:364–65.

22. *Works* 2:116, 255, 437; 21:174.

23. *Works* 17:376, 395–97, 401.

24. *Works* 21:172–73.

25. *Works* 22:130–35, 261.

26. *Works* 21:323; 2:394.

27. *Works* 25:520–21.

28. *Works* 12:254–55.

29. *Works* 2:187; 22:71. Italics added.

30. *Works* 6:365.

31. *Works* 13:336–37.

32. *Works* 13:336–37.

33. *Works* 2:98, 180.

34. *Works* 13:265.

35. *Works* 13:390.

36. *Works* 2:348; 21:184 He writes that the "fat of the innards" of Old Testament sacrifices "signified the love and obedience of the heart." It is a stretch from here to the realm of romantic attachments, but the image is vivid enough to mention. *Works* 20:60.

37. *Works* 20:481. The metaphor of the church as the bride of Christ is commonplace in the liturgy and literature of Christianity.

38. *Works* 13:247.

39. *Works* 22:135.

40. *Works* 21:172.

41. *Works* 2:410.

42. Cf. e.g. *Works* 2:116; 21:174; 12:253; 22:362.

43. *Works* 16:116; 13:466; 10:617.

44. *Works* 6:362–63.

45. *Works* 3:46.

46. *Works* 21:321–22.

47. *Works* 17:287; 2:187, 237–38, 410; 12:252.

48. *Works* 13:524; 22:363.

49. *Works* 22:170.

50. *Works* 16:416.

51. *Works* 17:288; 22:73.

52. *Works* 12:252–53.

53. *Works* 17:401.

54. *Works* 22:73, 119.

55. *Works* 25:520.

56. *Works* 2:208.

57. *Works* 14:102–8.

58. *Works* 19:82–85.

59. *Works* 17:376; 23:350–51.

60. *Works* 2:95, 106.

61. *Works* 2:114, 354.

62. *Works* 12:254.

63. *Works* 17:288–89.

64. *Works* 21:173.

65. *Works* 2:394.

66. *Works* 21:326–27.

67. *Works* 22:399.

68. *Works* 8:461.

69. *Works* 21:323; 8:461.

70. *Works* 2:241, 252–53.

71. *Works* 8:555, 253.

72. *Works* 2:108, 209, 254–63.

73. *Works* 17:314–15, 396–97.

74. *Works* 18:173.

75. *Works* 24:836; 22:71, 152.

76. *Works* 13:247, 416.

77. *Works* 24:950.

78. *Works* 24:1090–93; 3:226. These are chiefly comments on Paul's letters to the Ephesians and Galatians.

79. Cf. *Works* 18:77–78.

80. *Works* 25:519.

81. Stephen Stein notes a hateful, virulent tone in some of Edwards's biblical commentaries, particularly toward Catholics, and a certain relish at the agonies of the damned at the Last Judgment. Stein in *Works* 24:36–37, 84.

82. *Works* 25:519.

83. *Works* 16:109.

84. *Works* 24:1198; 2:289.

85. *Works* 13:416–17.

86. *Works* 19:82–85; 2:419; 3:141.

87. *Works* 21:175; 2:241, 252–53.

88. *Works* 8:184.

89. Marsden, *Edwards,* 370.

90. *Works* 15:200–201, 238, 371–77, 551, 583, 605; 24:616. Stephen Stein has a useful summary of Edwards's views on Solomon's reign in *Works* 5:40. For a stimulating discussion of Puritan imagery and language on this subject, see Mason Lowance, *The Language of Canaan* (Cambridge: Harvard University Press, 1980).

91. *Works* 24:616.

92. *Works* 15:538, 551, 583.

93. *Works* 15:238; 24:616.

94. McDermott, *One Holy,* 43ff. On the phenomenon in early Europe, see Norman Cohn, *The Pursuit of the Millennium: Revolutionary Millenarians and Mystical Anarchists of the Middle Ages* (Oxford: Oxford University Press, 1957). For the more recent U.S., see Paul Boyer, *When Time Shall Be No More: Prophecy Belief in Modern American Culture* (Cambridge: Harvard University Press, 1992). Edwards, well aware of the "ancient Gnostics and the wild fanatics" of the Reformation era, was a post-millennialist, who believed that

the Second Coming and Last Judgment would come after the Millennium, not before. Edwards, *Select Works* I:117. This differentiated him from many 17th-century and some early 18th-century Puritan ministers, including, for example, Increase and, more tentatively, Cotton Mather. Joy Gilsdorf, *The Puritan Apocalypse: New England Eschatology in the Seventeenth Century* (New York: Garland, 1989); James Davidson, *The Logic of Millennial Thought: Eighteenth-Century New England* (New Haven: Yale University Press, 1977). Edwards's view gained currency during and after the Great Awakening, an episode that some historians say made it easier for evangelical preachers to enter into the fervor surrounding the American Revolution. Cf. e.g. Alan Heimert, *Religion and the American Mind* (Cambridge: Harvard University Press, 1966), 27–94.

95. *Works* 13:369; 20:49.

96. *Works* 13:369.

97. *Works* 4:514.

98. Quoted in McDermott, *One Holy*, 69.

99. *Works* 9:471; 13:212.

100. *Works* 13:212–13.

101. *Works* 5:137–38, 337–38; 9:470.

102. *Works* 9:482–484; 5:40–41.

103. *Works* 9:484.

104. *Works* 9:482–83.

105. *Works* 5:137ff.

106. *Works* 13:427; 9:458–59.

107. Stein in *Works* 5:40.

108. *Works* 9:485.

109. *Works* 23:156.

110. *Works* 2:236.

111. *Works* 13:200, 483.

112. *Works* 17:253.

113. *Works* 13:369; 20:494.

114. Cf. John F. Wilson, "History, Redemption, and the Millennium," in Hatch and Stout, *Edwards and the American Experience*, 136–39. This essay stresses the extension of spiritual above technological advances as the way to the Millennium, although Edwards thought it would actually entail both.

115. *Works* 14:158.

116. Harry S. Stout depicts Edwards's Heaven in a slightly different way. Stout, "Edwards as Revivalist," in Stein, *Cambridge Companion*, 125ff.

117. *Works* 15:279.

118. *Works* 13:303.

119. *Works* 10:222; 17:72; 18:109; 9:499. See also Jenson, *America's Theologian*, 17.

120. *Works* 17:72.

121. *Works* 17:369–70.

122. *Works* 13:328–29.

123. *Works* 13:369.

124. *Works* 13:482.

125. *Works* 13:364–70.

126. *Works* 9:492.

127. *Works* 24:1066–67.

128. *Works* 10:392–93; 18:108–9.

129. *Works* 18:172.

130. *Works* 16:795.

131. *Works* 17:258–60.

132. Quoted in Murray, *Edwards,* 143.

133. *Works* 17:71; 22:304.

134. *Works* 13:201, 482.

135. *Works* 14:342; 13:202.

136. Ramsey in *Works* 8:98. Heaven, interestingly, is social well before the arrival of the saints on the Day of Judgment. Not only are the three entities of the Trinity there, but also an "innumerable company" of angels who constantly surround God. As Edwards describes them, projecting his social and political views and his reading of Scripture, angels are thoroughly social in nature. They are entities of power and dignity who exercise "superintendency" over the various parts of creation, including mankind's "different countries and kingdoms." They are ministers in the "affairs of God's dominion," immortal servants employed to fulfill and execute his will, "nobles and barons" in the palace of the king of kings. Dependent on God, they are destined to relinquish, to sanctified humans, their position of closeness to God in the ranks of the post-Apocalypse Heaven. Their position nonetheless allows them to "behold the face of the Father," and he theirs. Angels are very like humans in possessing "true virtue" and arraying themselves in "different degrees and ranks." Eventually they and the saints will form "one family" in communion with Christ. Like the nobility to the monarch, they may be God's companions as well as his minions. *Works* 13:186, 232, 284–85; 23:63, 182, 207. Edwards wrote quite a bit about angels in part because he wrote quite a bit about the book of Revelation, in which angels figure prominently.

137. *Works* 8:390–92.

138. *Works* 8:3, 61.

139. *Works* 8:378–79.

140. *Works* 8:381–82.

141. *Works* 8:383.

142. *Works* 8:385.

143. McDermott, *One Holy,* 91ff.

144. *Works* 8:396–97. For a somewhat different analysis, though reaching a similar conclusion, see Ronald Story, "Jonathan Edwards and the Gospel of Love," in Buckley, *A Place Called Paradise,* 91–106. "Paradise" here denotes the town of Northampton, not Heaven. For a sermon-length treatment, see Story, "Heaven Is a World of Love," in Hall, *Contribution,* 347–55.

Afterword

1. Marsden, *Edwards,* 337.

2. Miller, *Edwards,* 311.

3. *Works* 9:122. For a somewhat different view, see John E. Smith, "The Perennial Jonathan Edwards," in Lee and Guelzo, *Edwards in Our Times,* 1–11. Smith argues that Edwards acknowledged the validity of "profane" history and did not propose his Scripturally based history as a substitute, only as something of deeper meaning in a Hegelian sense. Smith, *Jonathan Edwards,* 135–35.

4. *Theodore Parker: An Anthology,* ed. Henry Steele Commager (Boston: Beacon Press, 1960), 131, 152.

5. Walter Rauschenbusch, *Christianity and the Social Crisis,* ed. Robert Cross (New York: Harper and Row, 1964; orig. published 1907), 246, 271.

6. Scholars have compared and contrasted Edwards and Emerson but not Edwards and Parker, and in the context of concern with beauty or nature or language, not charity. Cf. Miller, *Edwards,* 240; Michael McClymond, *Encounters with God: An Approach to the Theology of Jonathan Edwards* (Oxford: Oxford University Press, 1998), 123; David L. Weddle, "From Edwards to Emerson to Eddy: Extending a Trajectory of Metaphysical Idealism," in

Hall, *Contribution,* 128–46. One writer who did mention Edwards and Parker in the same breath was Harriet Beecher Stowe. Philip F. Gura, "Edwards and American Literature," in Stein, *Cambridge Companion,* 271. For brief but perceptive comments on Edwards and Rauschenbusch, see Michael J. McClymond, "A Different Legacy?", in Kling and Sweeney, *Jonathan Edwards at Home and Abroad,* 29–30.

7. On the development of institutionalized charity, see e.g. Conrad Edick Wright, *The Transformation of Charity in Postrevolutionary New England* (Boston: Northeastern University Press, 1992); and Peter Dobkin Hall's helpful review of Wright's book in *Nonprofit and Voluntary Sector Quarterly* (June 1997), 226–53, which contains an exemplary bibliography on the subject.

8. Robert H. Romer, *Slavery in the Connecticut Valley of Massachusetts* (Amherst: Levellers Press, 2009), 163, 204–5; Emilie Piper and David Levinson, *One Minute a Free Woman* (Great Barrington: Housatonic Press, 2010), 95–96, 104–5. Romer's meticulous research shows that most Connecticut Valley ministers of the mid-18th century owned slaves, including four of Edwards's Williams kinsmen; Yale and Harvard graduates were slave owners in nearly equal numbers. Also owning slaves were Benjamin Franklin; Cotton and Increase Mather; Edward Holyoke, and various Faneuils, Cabots, Bulfinches, and Endicotts; and Belchers as well as the Revolutionary heroes Benjamin Wadsworth, John Hancock, and Joseph Warren. It is unclear whether Solomon Stoddard did, although he apparently owned an indentured servant whom he bequeathed to his wife. Attitudes changed dramatically after the 1760s, underscoring the widely acknowledged point that both Enlightenment ideology and Christian morality were the keys to this change. Edwards does seem to have been more sensitive to the problem of slavery in free Christian society than some of his peers.

9. Roland A. Delattre, "Religious Ethics Today: Jonathan Edwards, H. Richard Niebuhr, and Beyond," in Lee and Guelzo, *Edwards in Our Time,* 67. On Edwards and slavery, see e.g. Marsden, *Edwards,* 255–58, 555; Charles E. Hambrick-Stowe, "All Things Were New and Astonishing: Edwardsian Piety, the New Divinity, and Race," in Kling and Sweeney, *Edwards at Home and Abroad,* 121–36; Kenneth P. Minkema, "Jonathan Edwards on Slavery and the Slave Trade," *William and Mary Quarterly* (October 1997), 823–30; John E. Smith, "The Perennial Jonathan Edwards," in Lee and Guelzo, *Edwards in Our Time,* 9. Anti-Catholicism, another strand of the antebellum benevolence movement, might also have found a champion in Edwards, who considered the Roman Catholic Church superstitious, authoritarian, and corrupt and a major impediment—the anti-Christ of Scripture—to the spread of the Reformed faith and the advent of the Millennium. Recent scholars find some evidence of ecumenical leanings in Edwards that might have bridged the Protestant-Catholic gulf, but the evidence is tenuous and the bridge in my view shaky. It is plausible to assume that Edwards would have eventually opposed slavery, Scripture notwithstanding. But there are profound differences between Protestantism and Roman Catholicism despite recent efforts to build a conservative political coalition of the two, and it is difficult to believe that Edwards, who built the structure of his faith and career partly on them, would not have found at least the non-violent aspects of the anti-Catholic crusade of considerable merit. Cf. Gerald R. McDermott, "A Possibility of Reconciliation: Jonathan Edwards and the Salvation of Non-Christians," in Lee and Guelzo, *Edwards in Our Time,* 173–202, which deals mainly with the possible salvation of heathens, a more tractable theoretical matter. Opposing slavery would represent a logical extension of charity for Edwards. Embracing Roman Catholicism would represent a capitulation to the bitterest enemies of his faith. This is hypothesis only, based on projecting patterns of Edwards's thought, which would certainly have changed dramatically by the mid-19th century. On recent political efforts on the conservative religious front, see e.g. Ronald Story and Bruce Laurie, *The Rise of Conservatism in America, 1945–2000* (Boston: Bedford/St. Martins, 2008).

10. Stein in Stein, *Cambridge Companion,* 5–7.

11. Cf. e.g. the portraits of Cotton Mather, Benjamin Colman, Thomas Foxcroft, Henry Flynt, Peter Bours, Jonathan Mayhew, John Lowell, Nathaniel Appleton, Daniel Greenleaf, Edward Holyoke, Charles Chauncy, and Mather Byles. Some of these may be seen online; most are reproduced in the volumes on colonial portraiture cited below. There are Anglicans as well as Congregationalists in the list, and sympathizers as well as adversaries of Edwards and the New Lights. Ministers faded quickly as portrait subjects after about 1760.

12. Wayne Craven makes a similar point about the merchant elite in *Colonial American Portraiture: The Economic, Religious, Social, Cultural, Philosophical, Scientific, and Aesthetic Foundations* (Cambridge: Cambridge, 1980).

13. The Whitefield portrait may be viewed online. The John Adams portrait, with biographical detail about Badger and an astute appraisal of his work as a portrait painter, is in Cuthbert Lee, *Early American Portrait Painters* (New Haven: Yale University Press, 1929), 196–206. For the "Two Children" picture, see Beatrix T. Rumford, ed., *American Folk Portraits* (New York: New York Graphic Society, 1981), 42. A color photograph of the portrait of Sarah Edwards is in Murray, *Edwards,* facing 192. Edwards may have agreed to sit for Badger because he did unpolished, near-primitive work, thus fitting Edwards's self-conception as an upholder of Puritan verities. There were also, on the other hand, few alternatives in 1751. The able if wooden John Smibert no longer did portraits because of failing eyesight; John Singleton Copley was still in his mid-teens. A sympathetic Scottish minister actually commissioned the portrait, but Edwards may have agreed to pose because, having been dismissed, he desired the sort of validation that a portrait could provide. This is sheer speculation, of little more value than trying to read Edwards's ideas and character from the Badger portrait.

Acknowledgments

The inspiration and encouragement of Kerry Buckley, Herbert Richardson, and Peter Ives were crucial in the initial stages of this project, as I have indicated in the preface. Dr. Buckley also reviewed portions of the manuscript for possible errors and made valuable comments in particular about Solomon Stoddard and colonial Northampton. Marie Panek of Historic Northampton read parts of the manuscript as well.

Paul Boller Jr., a longtime friend and my coeditor on other projects, sent ideas and suggestions early in the process and filled me in on the doings of various Edwards descendants. Peter Dobkin Hall, one of the preeminent scholars of American philanthropy, read a penultimate version and made encouraging, and much appreciated, noises.

Kenneth Minkema and Gerald McDermott, who have the Edwards canon and materials in their very bones, each critiqued the entire manuscript, catching factual mistakes and suggesting revisions of interpretation and phrasing. Dr. McDermott was also kind enough to share pre-publication chapters of a superb new work on Edwards's theology that he has cowritten with Michael McClymond, an act of immense and touching generosity.

Bruce Wilcox, Clark Dougan, and Carol Betsch at University of Massachusetts Press were unfailingly welcoming and professional in receiving this manuscript and shepherding it through the approval and editorial process, and I am grateful to Kay Scheuer for her meticulous copyediting.

I especially want to thank Dr. Laura Ricard, the most skillful editor I have ever known, an accomplished writer in her own right, and an authority on the religious history of colonial New England. Laura read drafts of every chapter as I finished them, discussed key interpretations, caught errors and omissions, and clarified the prose. If the book is in any degree cogent or compelling, much of the credit belongs to her unfailing critical eye and her encouragement. Without Laura Ricard this book would almost certainly not have seen the light.

All misstatements are of course my own.

General Index

Index of Edwards's Writings Mentioned by Title

RONALD STORY was born in Fort Worth, Texas, attended the University of Texas, worked for the U.S. government, and earned graduate degrees at Wisconsin and Stony Brook. In 1972 he joined the history department at the University of Massachusetts Amherst, where he taught courses in U.S. social and cultural history, the Civil War, and World War II until his retirement in 2006. Story is author, co-author, editor, or co-editor of *A More Perfect Union, The Forging of an Aristocracy, Sports in Massachusetts, Five Colleges, The Rise of American Conservatism, Generations of America, A Concise Historical Atlas of World War II,* and forty articles, essays, and digital products. He has served over the years as deacon of First Churches of Northampton, chair of the Amherst Democratic Town Committee, president of Historic Northampton, and coach of Amherst Little League baseball. He is currently writing a book on the artist George Biddle.